Ἡ Κλεὶς τῆς Γνώσεως

(The Key of the Sacred Science)

THE APOCALYPSE UNSEALED

BEING AN

ESOTERIC INTERPRETATION

OF

THE INITIATION OF IÔANNÊS

(᾿Αποκάλυψις ᾿Ιωάννου)

COMMONLY CALLED

THE REVELATION OF [ST.] JOHN

WITH A NEW TRANSLATION

BY

JAMES M. PRYSE

ὁ νικῶν

FIFTH EDITION

LOS ANGELES
JOHN M. PRYSE
LONDON
JOHN M. WATKINS
21 CECIL COURT, CHARING CROSS ROAD, W. C. 2

Entered at Stationers' Hall,
London.
(PRINTED IN THE U. S. A.)

LIST OF ILLUSTRATIONS

CONTENTS

PREFACE

The purpose of this book is to show that the *Apocalypse* is a manual of spiritual development and not, as conventionally interpreted, a cryptic history or prophecy. In the following pages the reader will find the complete solution of the Apocalyptic enigma, with ample proof of the correctness of that solution. As the subject dealt with in the work is, however, familiar to only a comparatively few special students of the sacred science, which to the many has ever been a sealed book, the exposition here given is put in the form of an elementary treatise. If it were written for the few, it would have been expanded to great bulk; but as it is intended for the many, the author has kept within the limits of a small volume, avoiding everything mystical, scholastic and controversial, using plain, concise language, and employing technical terms only when they are required by the nature of the subject.

The translation of the *Apocalypse* here presented attempts no more than to reproduce the meaning of the original accurately and clearly in modern English. But, while this translation differs radically, in some respects, from the authorized version, the interpretation here offered is not based upon any peculiarities of the translator's work, or upon any mere matter of details, but rests broadly upon the undisputed meanings of the Greek text.

JAMES M. PRYSE.

New York City, September, 1910.

Οὐαὶ ὑμῖν τοῖς νομικοῖς, ὅτι ἤρατε τῆν κλεῖδα τῆς γνώσεως· αὐτοὶ οὐκ εἰσήλθατε καὶ τοὺς εἰσερχομένους ἐκωλύσατε.

Woe unto you, conventionalists, for you took away the key of the sacred science; *you* did not go in and those who were about to go in you prevented. *Lk.* xi. 52

INTRODUCTION

CHAPTER I

THE KEY OF THE GNÔSIS

Every thoughtful student of the literature of the ancient religions, including that of early Christianity, can not but be impressed by the fact that in each and all of them may be found very clear intimations of a secret traditional lore, an arcane science, handed down from times immemorial. This secret body of knowledge is repeatedly alluded to in the *New Testament*, as also in the *Upanishads* and other ancient writings, in whose pages a few of the arcane doctrines are cautiously unveiled; and from the meagre glimpses thus afforded of the system it is clearly apparent that it was essentially the same in all the old religions and philosophies, constituting, in fact, their common esoteric basis. In the primitive Christian Church, organized as a secret society, this Gnôsis, or secret science, was guarded with jealous care, being imparted only to a comparative few who were deemed worthy of initiation, according to the maxim, "Many are the called, but few are the chosen." Through corrupting political influences and the ultimate dominance by a selfish and decadent priesthood, the Christian Society in the early centuries lost this esoteric knowledge, in place of which there grew up during the succeeding centuries a system of dogmatic theology formulated from the literal interpretation, the dead letter, of the books of the *Old* and *New Testaments*. On the hypothesis that the Bible, as a divine revelation, contains a record of God's dealings with mankind throughout the ages, the historical element in it has been unduly emphasized, while books that are purely allegorical and mystical have been construed as history. For several centuries it was attempted to give the *Apocalypse* an historical interpretation; and failing this, through the lack of any record of past events that would serve the purpose, it was next interpreted as history of the future, that is, prophecy. At the present time, the *Apocalypse* is the despair of theology; the ablest scholars in the ranks of orthodoxy frankly admit that it must be regarded as an unsolved, and possibly insoluble, enigma. They translate its title "Revelation"—yet it reveals nothing to them. Literally ἀποκάλυψις means "disrobing" or "unveiling"; but Isis wrapped in her *peplum* was not more safe from profane gaze than is the meaning of the *Apocalypse*, nor is any book in all literature more heavily veiled.

Yet the *Apocalypse* is the key to the *New Testament;* more, it is in very truth the key of the Gnôsis. Incomprehensible as the book may seem to the exoteric scholar, however great his intellectual attainments, keen his mental acumen, and vast his store of erudition, to the mere tyro in the sacred science the general meaning of the *Apocalypse* is perfectly clear. It is unintelligible to the conventional scholar simply because its subject-matter, veiled in symbolical language, relates to the Mysteries of the early Christian Society, the esoteric teachings which it was not lawful to reveal. For secrecy has always been maintained regarding the sacred science, so as to guard it from those who are morally unworthy to receive it; since the power its possession confers would be destructive to them and injurious to their fellow-men. But so far as concerns the *Apocalypse* this reason does not apply very forcibly: much that is given in it had already been very clearly and openly stated in the writings of Plato (with which the Apocalyptist was evidently familiar) and of other Greek Initiates, as well as in the Buddhistic and Brahmanical scriptures. Moreover, although the *Apocalypse* treats very fully of the spiritual and psychic forces in man, it nowhere gives even a clue to the process by which these forces can be aroused to action; in fact, in the introductory part Iôannês clearly intimates that it is intended for the guidance of those who, without any esoteric instruction, find these forces awakened within them by the very purity of their nature and the intensity of their aspiration for the spiritual life. Evidently, then, he had another motive for resorting to the symbology and the ingenious puzzles which have baffled the profane for so many centuries; and this motive is easily perceived. If he had written the book in clear language, it would almost undoubtedly have been destroyed; and it certainly would never have found a place in the Christian canon. Again, from the concluding portion of his *Evangel* it is plain that Iôannês, the great Seer and Initiate, clearly foresaw the fate of the Christian Church and its loss of the esoteric doctrine. It would seem, therefore, a reasonable supposition that he wrote the *Apocalypse* for the purpose of preserving that doctrine in the Christian records, carefully concealing it under the most extraordinary symbols, checked off by a numerical key and by similar "puzzles," so that the meanings could be conclusively demonstrated from the text itself, and concluding it with a dread imprecation against any one who should add to or take away anything from the book (a device which has undoubtedly helped to preserve the text from mutilation); and having thus with marvellous ingenuity prepared the book, which is unique in all literature, he confided it to the keeping of the exoteric church, confident that in their ignorance of the real nature of its contents the exotericists would carefully preserve it until the proper time should come for its meaning to be explained. If this was his purpose (as the present author firmly believes it was), then this present time, when modern Biblical criticism—scholarly accurate, conventionally exoteric, and remorselessly unsparing—has demonstrated the unsoundness and instability of the venerable theological structure, and has so undermined it that it seems to be tottering to its fall, would appear to be the intended and appropriate time for the seals of the *Apocalypse* to be broken, and the contents of the book made known. Thus it is that Iôannês, "who bore witness of the Logos of the God, and of the witness of Anointed Iêsous," has borne witness of the esoteric doctrine which underlies not only Christianity but also all the religions of antiquity.

Through the long centuries the orthodox church has treasured this mysterious book—designed for the undoing of orthodoxy—as part of its sacred scriptures, a place to which the book is justly entitled, for it is the masterpiece of Iôannês, the Seer. It is unquestionably from the same hand that penned the fourth *Evangel:* tradition is quite clear on that point; and though its Greek is somewhat inferior to that of the *Evangel,* the difference is due merely to the more intricate and artful composition of the *Apocalypse;* while both works reveal the same inimitable mental traits and unmistakable literary peculiarities. That they are by the same author, and that the text is practically intact, is the view of sober-minded Biblical scholars, a reaction having set in against an erratic school of criticism which is now generally discredited as being an instance of scholasticism running riot with untenable theories and whimsical conjectures.

Now, in plain words, what does this very occult book, the *Apocalypse,* contain? It gives the esoteric interpretation of the Christos-myth; it tells what "Iêsous the Christos" really is; it explains the nature of "the old serpent, who is the Devil and Satan"; it repudiates the profane conception of an anthropomorphic God; and with sublime imagery it points out the true and only path to Life Eternal. It gives the key to that divine Gnôsis which is the same in all ages, and superior to all faiths and philosophies—that secret science which is in reality secret only because it is hidden and locked in the inner nature of every man, however ignorant and humble, and none but himself can turn the key.

It is impossible for the Gnôsis itself ever to be "revealed," from the very nature of it, for it pertains to the realm of the spiritual mind, and lies beyond the scope of mere intellection, which can never rise higher than speculative philosophy; but the key of the Gnôsis—the scientific method by which this higher knowledge may be attained—can be placed in possession of any one who is intuitive enough to appreciate its value and apply it in practice.

CHAPTER II

THE PATH OF POWER

As but few readers may be expected to have sufficient acquaintance with ancient philosophy and the rather detailed knowledge of psycho-physiology necessary for even a superficial survey of the *Apocalypse,* a brief sketch will here be given of the topics which must be entered into in interpreting it. A comprehensive treatise, or even a complete outline of the subject, would be far beyond the scope of the present work, which is strictly limited to the elucidation of the *Apocalypse.*

The point where the arcane system sharply diverges from all the conventional schools of thought is in the means of acquiring knowledge. To make this clear, Plato's analysis of the four faculties of the soul, with their four corresponding degrees of knowledge, may be taken. (*Rep.* vi. 511.) Tabulated, it is as follows:

THE VISIBLE, SENSUOUS WORLD.

1. Εἰκασία, perception of images,	}	δόξα, opinion, illusory knowledge.
2. Πίστις, faith, psychic groping,		

THE INTELLIGIBLE, SUPRASENSUOUS WORLD.

3. Διάνοια, philosophic reason,	}	γνῶσις, ἐπιστήμη, wisdom, true knowledge.
4. Νόησις, direct cognition,		

The first of these degrees covers the whole field of the inductive physical sciences, which are concerned with investigating the phenomena of external nature; the second degree embraces exoteric religion and all phases of blind belief; and these two degrees, pertaining to the phrênic or lower mind, comprise all the knowledge available to those whose consciousness does not transcend the illusions of the material world. The third degree relates to speculative philosophy, which seeks to arrive at first principles by the effort of pure reason; the fourth degree is the direct apprehension of truth by the lucid mind independently of any reasoning process; and these two degrees, pertaining to the noetic or higher mind, represent the field of knowledge open to those whose consciousness rises to the world of spiritual reality. Elsewhere Plato speaks of the mantic state, which he describes as a kind of madness produced "by a divine release from the ordinary ways of men."

The exoteric scientist and religionist rely on the physical senses, the psychic emotions, and the intellectual faculties as these are in the present stage of human evolution; and while the scientist somewhat enlarges the scope of the senses by employing the telescope, the microscope, and other mechanical devices, the religionist puts his trust in the mutilated records of suppositional revelations received from the remote past. But the esotericist, refusing to be confined within the narrow limits of the senses and the mental faculties, and recognizing that the gnostic powers of the soul are hopelessly hampered and obscured by its imperfect instrument, the physical body, devotes himself to what may be termed intensive self-evolution, the conquest and utilization of all the forces and faculties that lie latent in that fontal essence within himself which is the primary source of all the elements and powers of his being, of all that he is, has been, and will be. By gaining conscious control of the hidden potencies which are the proximate causes of his individual evolution, he seeks to traverse in a comparatively brief period of time the path leading to spiritual illumination and liberation from terrestrial bondage, rushing forward, as it were, toward that goal which the human race as a whole, advancing at an almost imperceptible rate of progress, will reach only after æons of time. His effort is not so much to *know* as to *become;* and herein lies the tremendous import of the Delphic inscription, "Know Thyself," which is the key-note of esotericism. For the esotericist understands that true self-knowledge can be attained only through self-development in the highest possible sense of the term, a development which begins with introspection and the awakening of creative and regenerative forces which now slumber in man's inner protoplasmic nature, like the vivific potency in the ovum, and which when roused into activity transform him ultimately into a divine being bodied in a deathless ethereal form of ineffable beauty. This process of transcendental self-conquest, the giving birth to oneself as a spiritual being, evolving from the concealed essence of one's own embryonic nature a self-luminous immortal body, is the sole subject-matter of the *Apocalypse,* as it is also the burden of the four *Evangels;* but, whereas in his *Evangel* Iôannês has been content to follow the form of statement found in the three Synoptics, in the *Apocalypse* he has given an almost complete outline of the psycho-physiological process of regeneration or, as he calls it in his *Evangel,* the birth "from above."

In the esoteric philosophy—the infelicitous word esoteric being used in this work merely because the English language appears to afford no happier one—the absolute Deity is considered to be beyond the spheres of existence and ulterior to Being itself. The world of true Being is that of the Logos, or Nous, the realm of divine ideas, or archetypes, which are the eternal patterns, so to say, of all things in the manifested universe. By a paradox which defies the reasoning faculty, but which is readily resolved intuitively, the God is said to be apart from, and independent of the universe, and yet to permeate every atom of it. The God is the abstract Unit, which is the origin of all number, but which never loses its unit-value, and can not be divided into fractions; while the Logos is the manifested or collective Unit, a deific Individuality, the collectivity of a countless host of Logoi, who are differentiated into seven hierarchies, constituting in the aggregate the Second Logos, the uttered Thought, or Word.

As a mediate principle for the manifestation of the Logos in and from the God, Iôannês in his *Evangel* places the Archeus, the first element or substratum of substantive objectivity, that which becomes by differentiation first the subtile and then the gross material elements of the manifested worlds. If this primary substance is related back to the God, and considered as being prior to the Logos, the result is the refined dualism that mars some of the old systems of philosophy. But in the prologue the Logos is really coeval with the Archeus: the Logos *is* (subsists) in the Archeus, and the latter becomes, in the Logos, the principle of Life, which irradiates as Light. This Light of the Logos is identical with the Pneuma, the Breath or Holy Spirit, and esoterically it is the pristine force which underlies matter in every stage, and is the producer of all the phenomena of existence. It is the one force from which differentiate all the forces in the cosmos. As specialized in the human organism, it is termed, in the *New Testament*, the *paraklêtos*, the "Advocate," and is the regenerative force above referred to.

From the Archetypal world, that of the Logos, emanate successively the Psychic and the Material worlds; and to these three may be added a fourth, which is usually included, by ancient writers, in the Psychic, though in reality it is distinct from it. This fourth world, which will here be called the Phantasmal—since the word "hell" connotes misleading and lurid notions—is the region of phantoms, evil spirits, and psychic garbage generally.

All that the universe contains is contained also in man. The origin of man is in the Deity, and his true self or individuality is a Logos, a manifested God. Analogous with the universe or macrocosm, man, the microcosm, has three bodies, which are called in the *New Testament* the spiritual body (*sôma pneumatikon*), the psychic body (*sôma psychikon*), and the physical body (*sôma*, or *sarx*, "flesh"). In the *Upanishads* they are termed "causal body" (*kârana sharîra*), "subtile body" (*sûkshma sharîra*), and "gross body" (*sthûla sharîra*). In mystical writings they are made to correspond to the four occult elements, and also to the sun, moon, and earth, and hence are given the names air-body, water-body, fire-body, lunar body, and solar body. The spiritual (pneumatic) body is, strictly speaking, not a body at all, but only an ideal, archetypal form, ensphered, as it were, by the *pneuma* or primordial principle which in the duality of manifestation generates all forces and elements: it is therefore called the "causal body," because from its sphere all the other bodies are engendered; and all these lower forms are enveloped by the same circumambient aura (called in the *New Testament* "the radiance" or "glory," *hê doxa*), which is visible to the seer as an oviform faint film of bluish haze. Semi-latent within this pneumatic ovum is the paraklete, the light of the Logos, which in energizing becomes what may be described as living, conscious electricity, of incredible voltage and hardly comparable to the form of electricity known to the physicist. This is the "good serpent" of ancient symbology; and, taken with the pneumatic ovum, it was also represented in the familiar symbol of the egg and the serpent. It is called in the Sanskrit writings *kundalinî*, the annular or ring-form force, and in the Greek *speirêma*, the serpent-coil. It is this force which, in the telestic work, or cycle of initiation, weaves from the primal substance of the auric ovum, upon the ideal form or archetype it contains, and conforming thereto, the immortal Augoeidês, or solar body (*sôma hêliakon*), so called because in its visible appearance it is self-luminous like the sun, and has a golden radiance. Its aureola displays a filmy opalescence. This solar body is of atomic, non-molecular substance.

The psychic, or lunar, body, through which the Nous acts in the psychic world, is molecular in structure, but of far finer substance than the elements composing the gross physical form, to whose organism it closely corresponds, having organs of sight, hearing, and the rest. In appearance it has a silvery lustre, tinged with delicate violet; and its aura is of palest blue, with an interchanging play of all the prismatic colors, rendering it iridescent.

The physical body, in its physiological relation to psychology, will necessarily have to be considered somewhat in detail in elucidating the *Apocalypse;* but before entering on this subject, it may be explained that a fourth body is sometimes alluded to in mystical writings. It is called in Sanskrit *kâma rûpa*, the form engendered by lust, and it comes into existence only after the death of the physical body, save in the exceptional case of the extremely evil sorcerer who, though alive physically, has become morally dead. It is a phantasm shaped from the dregs and effluvia of matter by the image-creating power of the gross animal mind. Of such nature are the *daimones* and "unclean spirits" of the *New Testament*, where also the "abominable stench" (*bdelugma*) seems to be a covert allusion to this malodorous shade. This phantasm has the shadowy semblance of the physical body from which it was derived, and is surrounded by a cloudy aura of brick-red hue.

It should be observed that in the esoteric cosmogony the theory of "dead" matter has no place. The universe is a manifestation of life, of consciousness, from the Logos down to the very atoms of the material elements. But in this philosophy a sharp distinction is made between Being and existence: the Logos, the Archetypal world, is that of True Being, changeless and eternal; while existence is a going outward into the worlds of *becoming*, of ceaseless change and transformation. The Nous, the immortal man, or mind (for the mind should be regarded as the real man), when incarnated comes under the sway of this law of mutation, entering upon a long cycle of incarnations, passing from one mortal body to another. The metaphysical aspect of this subject need not be discussed here; but it may be said that the fact of reincarnation, so far from being mysterious and difficult of proof, is really very prosaic and simple, so that it has always been treated as exoteric in all archaic religions and philosophies. Positive knowledge of its truth, on a basis of personal experience, is one of the first results obtained by any one who enters upon the initial stages of self-conquest. It is then a fact as apparent to him as are the cognate facts of birth and death. The telestic work has for its object to achieve deliverance from reincarnation, and this deliverance is complete and final only when the deathless solar body is formed, and the perfected man is thereby freed from the necessity of reincarnating in the mortal physical and psychic forms.

The physical body may itself be considered to be an objective microcosm, an epitome of the material world, to every department of which its organs and functions correspond and are in direct relation. Moreover, as the organism through which the soul contacts external nature, its organs correspond to, and are the respective instruments of, the powers and faculties of the soul. Thus the body has four principal life-centres which are, roughly speaking, analogues of the four worlds, and of the four manifested generic powers of the soul; these four somatic divisions are as follows:

1. The head, or brain, is the organ of the Nous, or higher mind.

2. The region of the heart, including all the organs above the diaphragm, is the seat of the lower mind (*phrên,* or *thumos*), including the psychic nature.

3. The region of the navel is the centre of the passional nature (*epithumia*), comprising the emotions, desires, appetites, and passions.

4. The procreative centre is the seat of the vivifying forces on the lowest plane of existence. This

centre is often ignored by ancient writers as, for instance, Plato, who assigns four faculties to the soul, but classifies only three of the somatic divisions, assigning the Nous, or Logos, to the head, *thumos* to the cardiac region, and *epithumia* to the region below the midriff. Others, however, give the fourfold system, as does Philolaus, the Pythagorean, who placed the seat and germ (*archê*) of reason in the head, that of the psychic principle in the heart, that of growth and germination in the navel, and that of seed and generation in the sexual parts.

It is unnecessary, in this brief sketch, to go into further details concerning these correspondences, save only in regard to the nervous system and the forces operating through it. There are two nervous structures: the cerebro-spinal, consisting of the brain and the spinal cord; and the sympathetic or ganglionic system. These two structures are virtually distinct yet intimately associated in their ramifications. The sympathetic system consists of a series of distinct nerve-centres, or ganglia—small masses of vascular neurine—extending on each side of the spinal column from the head to the coccyx. Some knowledge of these ganglia and the forces associated with them is indispensable in an examination into the meaning of the *Apocalypse;* and as their occult nature is more fully elucidated in the *Upanishads* than in any other available ancient works, the teaching therein contained will here be referred to, and their Sanskrit terms employed. The ganglia are called *chakras,* "discs," and forty-nine of them are counted, of which the seven principal ones are the following: (1) sacral ganglion, *mûlâ-*

dhâra; (2) prostatic, *adhishthâna;* (3) epigastric, *manipuraka;* (4) cardiac, *anâhata;* (5) pharyngeal, *vishuddhi;* (6) cavernous, *âjñâ;* and (7) the conarium, *sahasrâra.* Of these only the seventh, the conarium or pineal body, need be considered here with particularity. It is a small conical, dark-grey body situated in the brain immediately behind the extremity of the third ventricle, in a groove between the nates, and above a cavity filled with sabulous matter composed of phosphate and of carbonate of lime. It is supposed by modern anatomists to be the vestige of an atrophied eye, and hence is termed by them "the unpaired eye." Though atrophied physically, it is still the organ of spiritual vision when its higher function is restored by the vivifying force of the *speirêma*, or paraklete, and it is therefore called esoterically "the third eye," the eye of the seer.

When through the action of man's spiritual will, whether by his conscious effort or unconsciously so far as his phrênic mind is concerned, the latent *kundalinî* (*speirêma*), which in the *Upanishads* is poetically said to lie coiled up like a slumbering serpent, is aroused to activity, it displaces the slow-moving nervous force or neuricity and becomes the agent of the telestic or perfecting work. As it passes from one ganglion to another its voltage is raised, the ganglia being like so many electric cells coupled for intensity; and moreover in each ganglion, or *chakra*, it liberates and partakes of the quality peculiar to that centre, and it is then said to "conquer" the *chakra*. In Sanskrit mystical literature very great stress is laid upon this "conquering of the *chakras*."

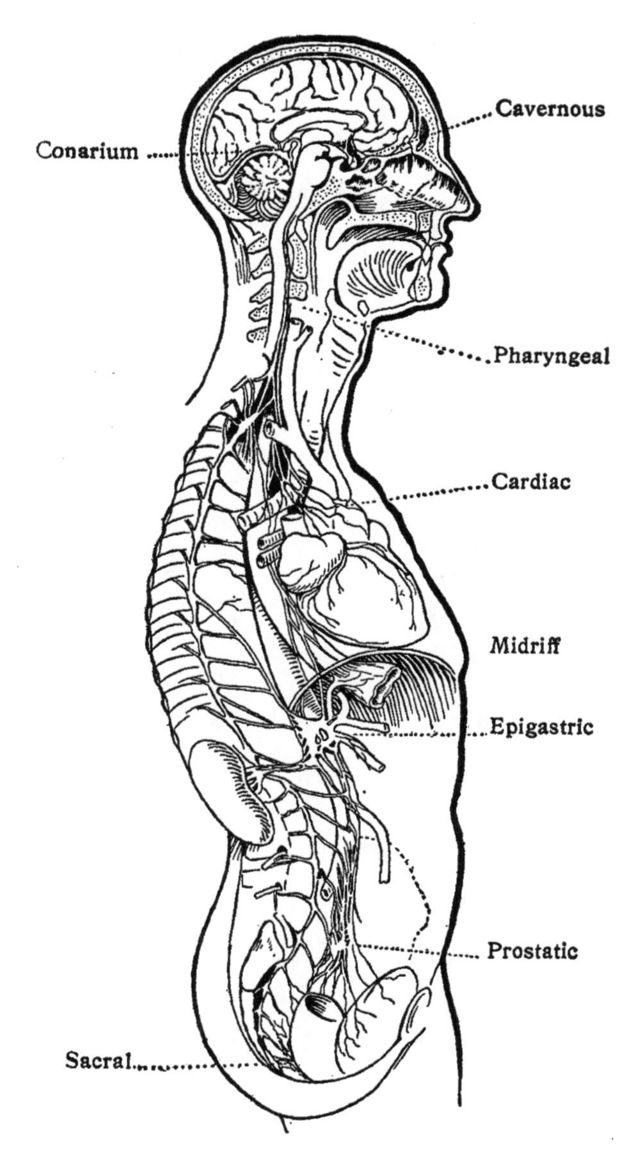

The Seven Principal Ganglia

The currents of the *kundalinî,* as also the channels they pursue, are called *nâdîs,* "pipes" or "tubes," and the three principal ones are: (1) *sushumnâ,* which passes from the terminus of the spinal cord to the top of the cranium, at a point termed the *brahmarandra,* or "door of Brahma" (in early Christian mysticism, *thura Iêsou,* "door of Iêsous"); (2) *pingala,* which corresponds to the right sympathetic; and (3) *îdâ,* which corresponds to the left sympathetic. The force, as specialized in the ganglionic system, becomes the seven *tattvas,* which in the *Apocalypse* are called the seven *pneumata,* "breaths," since they are differentiations of the Great Breath, the "World-Mother," symbolized by the moon. Concurrent with these seven lunar forces are five solar forces pertaining to the cerebrospinal system, called the five *prânas,* "vital airs," or "life-winds," which in the *Apocalypse* are termed "winds" (*anemoi*). The *Apocalypse* represents these twelve forces, the seven "breaths" and the five "winds," as corresponding to the twelve signs of the zodiac, of which, therefore, a brief description will here be appropriate.

The zodiac is a belt of the celestial sphere, about seventeen degrees in breadth, containing the twelve constellations which the sun traverses during the year in passing around the ecliptic. Within this zone are confined the apparent motions of the moon and major planets. The zodiacal circle was divided by the ancients into twelve equal portions called signs, which were designated by the names of the constellations then adjacent to them in the following order: Aries, the Ram; Taurus, the Bull; Gemini, the Twins; Cancer, the Crab; Leo, the Lion; Virgo, the Virgin; Libra, the Balance; Scorpio, the Scorpion; Sagittarius, the Bowman; Capricornus, the Goat; Aquarius, the Water-bearer; and Pisces, the Fishes. Owing to the precession of the equinoxes, the signs of the ecliptic are now about one place

The Twelve Signs of the Zodiac

ahead of the corresponding zodiacal constellations, which constitute the fixed zodiac. Aside from its astronomical utility, the scheme of the zodiac was employed to symbolize the relations between the macrocosm and the microcosm, each of the twelve signs being made to correspond to one of the twelve greater gods of the ancient pantheon and assigned as the "house" of one of the seven sacred planets;

each sign, moreover, being said to govern a particular portion of the human body, as shown in the familiar exoteric chart here reproduced.

The foregoing covers the topics which must necessarily be referred to in elucidating the recondite meaning of the *Apocalypse;* but to convey a clearer conception of its practical and psychological application, further explanation will now be given of the action of the "serpent force" (*speirêma*) in the telestic or perfective work. This work has to be preceded by the most rigid purificatory discipline, which includes strict celibacy and abstemiousness, and it is possible only for the man or woman who has attained a very high state of mental and physical purity. To the man who is gross and sensual, or whose mind is sullied by evil thoughts or constricted by bigotry, the holy paraklete does not come; the unpurified person who rashly attempts to invade the adytum of his inner God can arouse only the lower psychic forces of his animal nature, forces which are cruelly destructive and never regenerative. The neophyte who has acquired the "purifying virtues" before entering upon the systematic course of introspective meditation by which the spiritual forces are awakened, must also as a necessary preliminary gain almost complete mastery of his thoughts, with the ability to focus his mind undeviatingly upon a single detached idea or abstract concept, excluding from the mental field all associated ideas and irrelevant notions. If successful in this mystic meditation, he eventually obtains the power of arousing the *speirêma,* or paraklete, and can thereby at will enter into the state of *manteia,* the sacred trance of seership. The four mantic states are not psychic trances or somnambulic conditions; they pertain to the noetic, spiritual nature; and in every stage of the *manteia* complete consciousness and self-command are retained, whereas the psychic trances rarely transcend the animalistic phrênic nature, and are usually accompanied by unconsciousness or semi-consciousness.

Proficiency in the noetic contemplation, with the arousing of the *speirêma* and the conquest of the life-centres, leads to knowledge of spiritual realities (the science of which constitutes the Gnôsis), and the acquirement of certain mystic powers, and it culminates in emancipation from physical existence through the "birth from above" when the deathless solar body has been fully formed. This telestic work requires the unremitting effort of many years, not in one life only but carried on through a series of incarnations until the final result is achieved. But almost in its initial stages the consciousness of the aspirant becomes disengaged from the mortal phrênic mind and centred in the immortal noetic mind, so that from incarnation to incarnation his memory carries over, more or less clearly according to the degree he has attained, the knowledge acquired; and with this unbroken memory and certainty of knowledge he is in truth immortal even before his final liberation from the cycle of reincarnation.

In arousing the *kundalinî* by conscious effort in meditation, the *sushumnâ*, though it is the all-important force, is ignored, and the mind is concentrated upon the two side-currents; for the *sushumnâ* can not be energized alone, and it does not start into activity until the *îdâ* and the *pingala* have preceded it, forming a positive and a negative current along the spinal cord. These two currents, on reaching the sixth *chakra*, situated back of the nasal passages, radiate to the right and left, along the line of the eyebrows; then the *sushumnâ*, starting at the base of the spinal cord, proceeds along the spinal marrow, its passage through each section thereof corresponding to a sympathetic ganglion being accompanied by a violent shock, or rushing sensation, due to the accession of force—increased "voltage"—until it reaches the conarium, and thence passes outward through the *brahmarandra*, the three currents thus forming a *cross* in the brain. In the initial stage the seven psychic colors are seen, and when the *sushumnâ* impinges upon the brain there follows the lofty consciousness of the seer, whose mystic "third eye" now becomes, as it has been poetically expressed, "a window into space." In the next stage, as the brain-centres are successively "raised from the dead" by the serpent-force, the seven "spiritual sounds" are heard in the tense and vibrant aura of the seer. In the succeeding stage, sight and hearing become blended into a single sense, by which colors are heard, and sounds are seen—or, to word it differently, color and sound become one, and are perceived by a sense that is neither sight nor hearing but both. Similarly, the psychic senses of taste and smell become unified; and next the two senses thus reduced from the four are merged in the interior, intimate sense of touch, which in turn vanishes into the epistemonic faculty.

the gnostic power of the seer—exalted above all sense-perception—to cognize eternal realities. This is the sacred trance called in Sanskrit *samâdhi,* and in Greek *manteia;* and in the ancient literature of both these languages four such trances are spoken of. These stages of seership, however, are but the beginning of the telestic labor, the culmination of which is, as already explained, rebirth in the imperishable solar body. As the *Apocalypse* has for its sole theme this spiritual rebirth, it should now be apparent why that book has ever been unintelligible to the conventional theologian, and has never yielded its secrets to the mere man of letters.

CHAPTER III

THE RIDDLES OF "REVELATION"

In the analysis which will be given in the next chapter it will be shown that the *Apocalypse* is a coherent whole, symmetrical, and having every detail fitted into its appropriate place with studied care. In its orderly arrangement and concise statement the book is a model of precise literary workmanship. But it contains a series of elaborate puzzles, some of which are based upon the numerical values of certain Greek words, thereby serving to verify the correct interpretation of the more important symbols; and as the detailed explanation of these in the analysis would interrupt the interpretation of the book as a whole, for the sake of clearness the solution of these puzzles will here be given in advance.

In the *Apocalypse* four animal-symbols or beasts (*thêria*) are conspicuous *dramatis personæ:* (1) a Lamb, having seven horns and seven eyes, and who is identified as Iêsous, who becomes "the Conqueror"; (2) a beast resembling a Leopard, with a bear's feet and a lion's mouth, and having seven heads and ten horns; (3) a red Dragon, having seven heads and ten horns, and who is "the Devil and Satan"; and (4) a beast having two horns like a Lamb but speaking like a Dragon, and who is called the Pseudo-Seer, or false teacher (*pseudo-prophêtês*). Of these four the Leopard is particularly referred to as "the Beast"; and concerning him the Apocalyptist says:

"Here is cleverness (*sophia*): he who has the Nous, let him count the number of the Beast; for it is the number of a man, and his number is 666."

The "cleverness" of this puzzle lies in its very simplicity; for the words "the Nous" (ὁ νοῦς), the familiar term in Greek philosophy for the higher mind, or man, naturally suggest the correct answer, the Phrên (ἡ φρήν), the cognate term for the lower mind, or man. As numbers are expressed in Greek by the letters of the alphabet, and not by arithmetical figures, the number of a name is simply the sum of the numerical values of the letters composing it. Thus the numerical value of *hê phrên* is 666. If this were the whole of the puzzle, it would be almost puerile; but it is, in fact, only a part of, and the clue to, an elaborate puzzle, which in its entirety is remarkably ingenious. It will be noticed that the

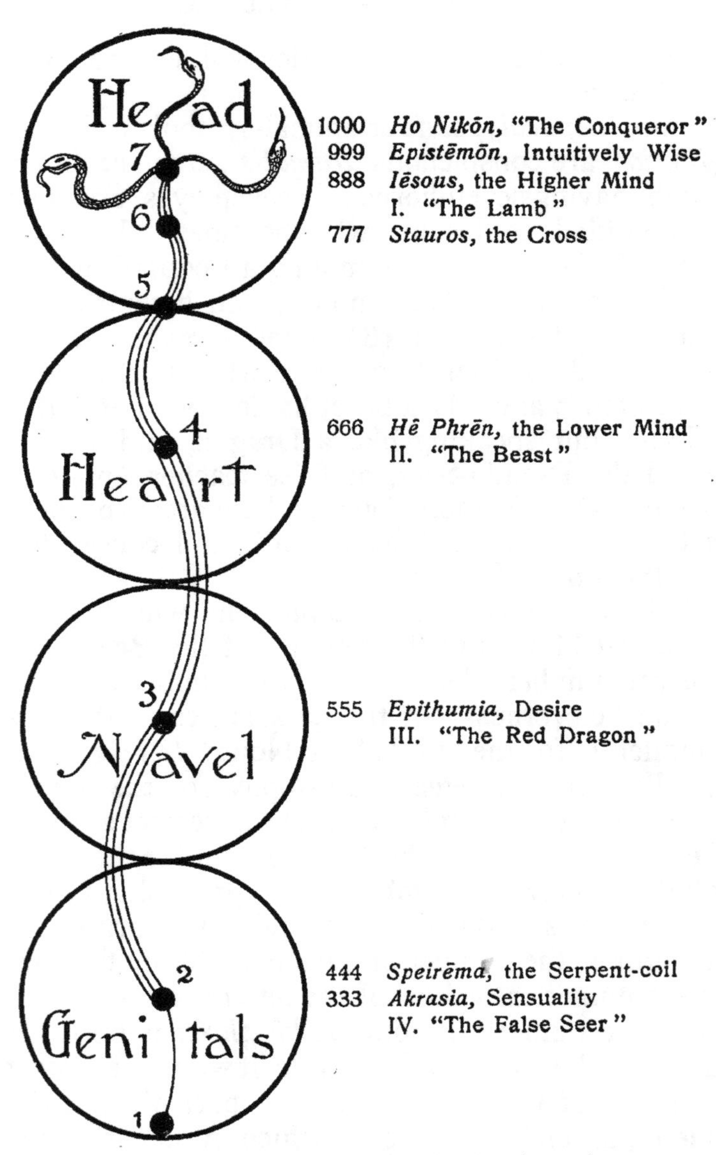

The Gnostic Chart Concealed in the Apocalypse

1. The Conqueror (*ho nikōn*)

Letter	Value
ὁ	70
ν	50
ι	10
κ	20
ω	800
ν	50
	1,000

2. Intuitively Wise (*epistēmōn*)

Letter	Value
ἐ	5
π	80
ι	10
στ	6
η	8
μ	40
ω	800
ν	50
	999

3. The Higher Mind (*Iēsous*)

Letter	Value
Ἰ	10
η	8
σ	200
ο	70
υ	400
ς	200
	888

4. The Cross (*stauros*)

Letter	Value
στ	6
α	1
υ	400
ρ	100
ο	70
ς	200
	777

5. The Lower Mind (*hē phrēn*)

Letter	Value
ἡ	8
φ	500
ρ	100
η	8
ν	50
	666

6. Desire (*epithumia*)

Letter	Value
ἐ	5
π	80
ι	10
θ	9
υ	400
μ	40
ι	10
α	1
	555

7. The Serpent-coil (*speirēma*)

Letter	Value
σ	200
π	80
ε	5
ι	10
ρ	100
η	8
μ	40
α	1
	444

8. Incontinence (*akrasia*)

Letter	Value
ἀ	1
κ	20
ρ	100
α	1
σ	200
ι	10
α	1
	333

(8.) Licentiousness (*akolasia*)

Letter	Value
ἀ	1
κ	20
ο	70
λ	30
α	1
σ	200
ι	10
α	1
	333

The Numbers of the Names

Beast, the phrênic mind, is the faculty ruling over one of the four somatic divisions, from which the natural inference is drawn that the three other beasts likewise are the regents of the three other somatic divisions. The Lamb, Iêsous, would therefore stand for the highest of these, the Nous. Now, the word *Iêsous* gives the sum 888. The red Dragon, "the archaic serpent, who is the Devil and Satan," fits neatly into place as the ruler of the third somatic division, *epithumia,* which word yields the number 555. The fourth beast, the "False Prophet," takes his place in the fourth division as the generative principle, *akrasia,* "sensuality," the number of his name being 333. Plato applies to this principle the word *akolasia,* which has the same meaning and the same numerical value.

Placing these four names, with their numbers, in the form of a diagram of the four somatic divisions, it becomes apparent that the puzzle is still only partly solved, for evidently a complete series of numbers is intended. A space is left where the diagram, to fill out the meaning, requires the cross, and another space for the "good serpent," the regenerative force; the "bad serpent," the Devil, the lust for life which leads to generation, being already included. The number of the cross, *stauros,* is 777 (the letters στ being taken, of course, as ϛ=6). The spiraling electric force, "the coil of the serpent," is the *speirêma,* which word gives the number 444. Now, the action of this force upon the brain, where its triple current forms the cross, gives the noetic perception, direct cognition (the *epistêmê,* or highest degree of knowledge, so beautifully defined by Plato), and to express this in the diagram it becomes necessary to insert the word *epistêmôn,* the philosophic and esoteric equivalent for the exoteric word *christos;* its numerical value is 999. Further, he who has attained to this higher knowledge forthwith becomes the conqueror, and as "The Conqueror" is the hero, so to say, of the Apocalyptic Drama, his name must be placed at the head of the list, as *ho nikôn,* with its number, 1,000.

The diagram thus completed makes clear the basic teaching of the *Apocalypse,* which treats of the *speirêma* and its energizing through the vital centres as the Conqueror gains mastery over them and builds up for himself, out of that primordial substance, his immortal vehicle, the monogenetic or solar body. This deathless solar vesture is symbolized as a city which comes down out of the sky, enveloped in the radiance (*doxa*) of the God, and it is portrayed with poetic imagery of exquisite beauty. The description, with its wealth of detail, should be enough to show very clearly what the city really is; but Iôannês has supplied conclusive proof of the true meaning by inserting in the description a puzzle which reads as follows:

"The Divinity who was talking with me had for a measure a golden reed, to measure the city, its gateways, and its wall. The city lies foursquare, and its length is as great as the width. He measured the city with the reed, by *stadia,* twelve thousand; its length, width and height are equal. And he measured its wall, one hundred and forty-four cubits, [including] the measure of a man, that is, of a Divinity."

As the expression "by *stadia*" (ἐπὶ σταδίων) shows that the measurement should not be taken in *stadia,* it naturally follows that it should be reduced to miles. Therefore, dividing 12,000 by 7½, the number of *stadia* to the Jewish mile, the quotient is 1,600, and this is the numerical value of the words *to sôma hêliakon,* "the solar body." In the authorized version the prepositon *epi,* "by," is not translated, being omitted as redundant—which merely shows the untrustworthiness of an empirical translation. That version also reads, "a hundred and forty and four cubits, [according to] the measure of a man, that is, of an angel," the inserted words making the passage meaningless. The "wall" of the solar body is its aura, or "radiance," *hê doxa;* but the letters of that name amount to only 143. As a puzzle, that number would be too transparent, nor would it harmonize with the other numbers given in relation to the city, as the twelve thousand *stadia,* twelve gateways, twelve foundations, etc., all of which have a real or an apparent reference to the zodiac. Therefore Iôannês increased it to 144, the square of twelve, by adding another *alpha,* which he calls "the measure of a man, that is, of a Divinity." In the formula, "I am the *Alpha* and the *Ô* [*mega*], the first and the last," *alpha* is the symbol of the divine man, or Divinity, before his fall into matter; and *ô mega* is the symbol of the perfected man, who has passed through the cycle of reincarnation and regained the spiritual consciousness.

The city is described as having the form of a cube. To solve this element of the puzzle it is only

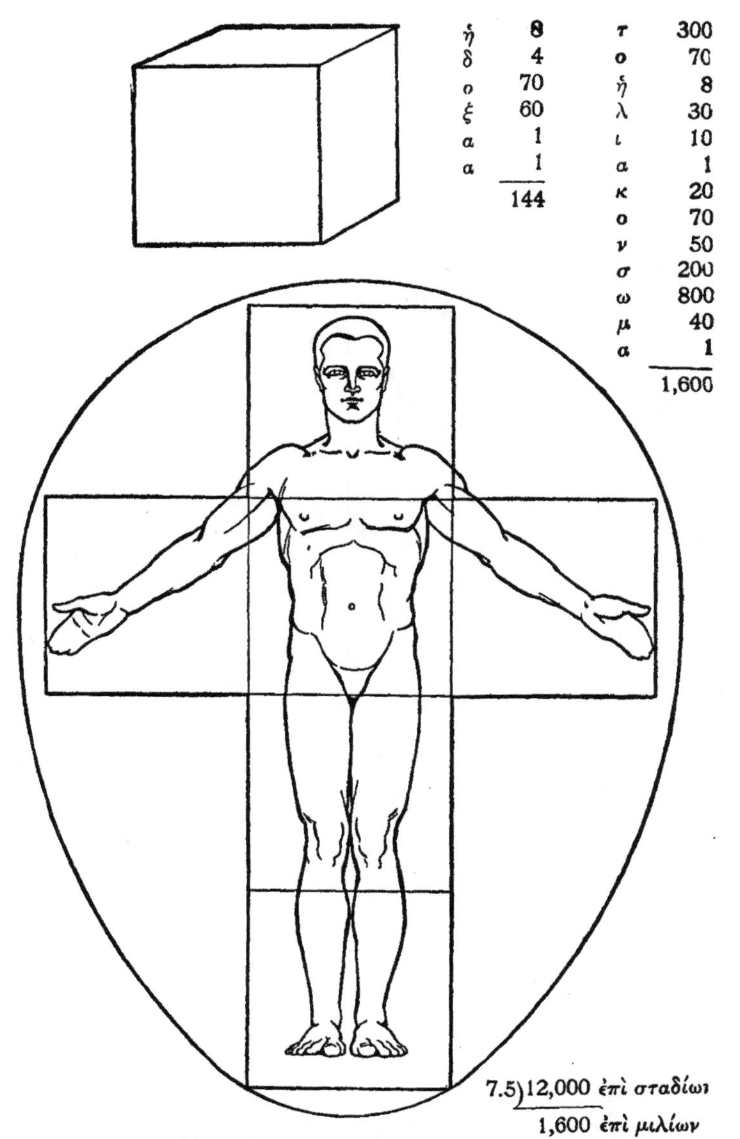

The Cubical City Unfolded

necessary to *unfold* the cube, thereby disclosing a cross, which represents the human form—a man with outstretched arms.

Although Iôannês speaks of measuring "the city, its gateways, and its wall," he does not give the measure of the gateways, for the very obvious reason that it is wholly unnecessary, since the word "gateway" (*pylôn*, from *pylê*, "an orifice") sufficiently indicates their nature: they are the twelve orifices of the body. In the *Upanishads* the human body is often called poetically the twelve-gate city of God's abode.

CHAPTER IV

THE DRAMA OF SELF-CONQUEST

In literary construction the *Apocalypse* follows to some extent the conventional model of the Greek drama: although in narrative form, it divides naturally into acts, or scenes, in each of which the scenic setting is vividly pictured; and interspersed with the action are monologues, dialogues, and choruses, and even the *deus-ex-machina*, or "god-on-a-string," plays a part. As a mere literary device, these scenes are represented in a series of visions; and in this Iôannês has adopted the style of the Hebrew seers, from whom he obtained much of the quaint symbolism, ornate imagery, and mystifying phraseology he employs, having as full right to them, doubtless, as the older seers had, for their curious symbology and cryptic jargon appear to have been the common property of the *nabia*, who had their initiation in the schools of seership. But with the material obtained from this source Iôannês has skilfully combined symbols drawn from the pagan Greek and the Christian *arcana,* even levying, it would seem, upon the Egyptian, Chaldaic and other systems, weaving these materials into a harmonious whole, wonderfully systematic and complete, and having all the details worked out with painstaking exactness. Then, having thus darkly veiled his teachings by this eclectic symbolism, utterly baffling to the conventional symbologist, he has ingeniously supplied means for verifying the import of each of the principal symbols, and this he accomplished by word-numbers and other puzzles.

By sentimental literalists the *Apocalypse* is generally accepted as a record of visions actually seen by "the Seer of Patmos," although it requires but little discrimination to perceive that the visionary style is merely an artifice of the Apocalyptist, adopted for the purpose of introducing the fabulous characters of his drama and mystifying his readers. It is only the psychics, the *mystai* or "veiled ones," who see symbolical visions. The true seer, the *epoptês,* beholds the things of nature and of supranature as they really *are,* and not as they *seem:* perceiving that all the forms and processes of external nature are themselves but the shadowy symbols of the eternal Ideas of the intelligible world, he passes beyond this fabric of material and psychic glamour, this veil by which the True is covered and concealed, and penetrates to the first principles of things, the archetypal, spiritual realities.

A few of the technical words employed by the *New Testament* writers are substitutes for terms used in older Greek. Thus *angelos*, "messenger," takes the place of the word *daimôn*, Deity in manifestation, including the hosts of lesser deities, powers and essences. As the anglicized word "angel" summons to the mind only the theological and popular conception of a celestial being whose function in the universe is undetermined and dubious, *angelos* will in this work be rendered "Divinity," a word which covers in range of meanings the various significations of the Greek word. Similarly, *apokalypsis*, literally, "uncovering," "unveiling," is a substitute for *epopteia*, "beholding," a word technically denoting initiation into the greater mysteries. The *Apocalypse* is, as its title implies, an account of the initiation of Iôannês himself. In the subtitle he calls it "the Initiation of Anointed Iêsous," that is, of his own illumined Nous, the "witness" for the universal Logos, as Iôannês in the material world, the "slave" (*doulos*) of the true Self, is the "witness" for the individual Logos.

Many actors, apparently, play their parts in the drama of the *Apocalypse;* yet in reality there is but one performer—the neophyte himself, the sacrificial "Lamb," who awakens all the slumbering forces of his inner nature, passes through the terrible ordeals of the purificatory discipline and the telestic labors, and finally emerges as the Conqueror, the self-perfected Man who has regained his standing among the deathless Gods. He is the hero of, and the sole actor in the drama; all the other *dramatis personæ* are only personifications of the principles, faculties, forces, and elements of Man, that minor world so vast and mysterious, whose ultimate destiny it is to become coëxtensive with the divine and illimitable universe.

In the brief prologue to the drama, the Anointed Iêsous, the illuminated Mind, is depicted as the first-born from the dead (the moribund inner faculties), the ruler of the lower powers, yet having been crucified by them on the cross of matter, the physical body. Now, at his coming, they who wounded him shall weep and wail over him. In the *New Testament* allegory there are two crucifixions: one relating to the soul's descent into matter, the generation of the physical form, and the other to its ascent to spirit, or regeneration in the solar body.

Then, "in the Breath," that is, in *samâdhi,* the sacred trance, Iôannês has a vision of the Logos, his own spiritual Self, in the self-luminous pneumatic body, of which he gives a magnificent description, partly literal and partly symbolical. He sees him walking to and fro among seven little lampstands, and holding in his right hand seven stars; announcing himself to be the ever-living Self, who became "dead" (incarnated), but is now alive throughout the æons, the Logos explains that the lampstands are the "seven Societies in Asia," and the seven stars their Divinities. That is, they represent respectively the seven Rays of the Light of the Logos (his seven forces), and the seven centres or *chakras* in the body, through which they energize. Asia is the native land of Iôannês, therefore typifying the body, the home-land of the soul; and the seven Societies (groups or ganglia) are designated by the names of Asian cities, each of which, by some well-known characteristic, or something for which it was noted, calls to mind the somatic centre it represents. These cities are given in the same order in the *Apocalypse* as are the *chakras* in the *Upanishads*, thus: (1) *Mûlâdhâra,* sacral ganglion; Ephesos, a city celebrated for its great temple of Diana, the "many-breasted mother," who appears in the *Apocalypse* as the "Woman clothed with the Sun, the moon underneath her feet," the lunar goddess and the Apocalyptic heroine alike personifying the regenerative force, the *sushumnâ,* mystically called the "World-Mother." (2) *Adhishthâna,* prostatic ganglion; Smyrna, noted for the fig industry; the fig is preëminently a phallic symbol. (3) *Manipuraka,* epigastric ganglion; Pergamos, celebrated for its temple of Æsculapius; the epigastric, or solar plexus, is the controlling centre of the vital processes of the body, and of the forces utilized in all systems of psychic healing. (4) *Anâhata,* cardiac ganglion; Thyateira, a city noted for the manufacture of scarlet dyes; the name being thus a covert reference to the blood and the circulatory system. (5) *Vishuddhi,* laryngeal ganglion; Sardeis, a name which suggests the *sardion,* sardine or carnelian, a flesh-colored stone, thus alluding to the laryngeal protuberance vulgarly termed "Adam's apple." (6) *Âjñâ,* cavernous ganglion; Philadelpheia, a city which was repeatedly destroyed by earthquakes; the manifestation of the *kundalinî* at this sixth centre is especially violent, and so Iôannês describes the opening of the sixth seal (which is identical with the sixth Society) as being accompanied by a "great earthquake." (7) *Sahasrâra,* conarium, or pineal body, the "third eye"; Laodikeia, noted for the manufacture of the so-called "Phrygian powder," which was esteemed a sovereign remedy for sore and weak eyes, presumably the "eyesalve" mentioned by Iôannês in the message to this seventh Society.

To each of these Societies the Logos sends a message; and in these communications, which he dictates to Iôannês, the nature and function of each centre is indicated: a particular aspect of the Logos is presented to each one, a good and a bad quality being ascribed to each centre, and a reward or prize is promised, specifying the spiritual results accruing to "the Conqueror" from the conquest of each *chakra.*

In the next vision is shown the Logos enthroned in the sky, with his four septenary powers. Here Iôannês has constructed a simple little puzzle by employing redundant symbols and by inverting the order of the forces, enumerating the lesser ones first and the greater ones last. He places twenty-four Ancients ("elders") circling the throne, before which also are seven Breaths ("spirits") and a crystalline sea; after which he describes four *Zôa* ("living creatures"), each of whom has six wings. Yet he makes it clearly apparent, later, that the *Zôa* are superior to the Ancients and next in rank to the Logos. In fact, the four *Zôa* are the four manifested Powers of the Logos, the archetypes of the four "Beasts," whose nature, as the regents of the four somatic divisions, has already been explained. As these *Zôa* are septenates, they are said to have six wings each. These wings are identical with the twenty-four Ancients; and the seven Breaths before the throne are likewise identical with the highest septenate, the noetic *Zôon*. The seemingly complicated assemblage thus resolves itself simply into the Nous centred in the brain, with its four septenary powers; and the "glassy sea" is the ether pulsating in the mystic "eye" of the seer. For the "sky" in the *Apocalypse* is not the "heaven" of the profane, the celestial world supposed by them to be somewhere in the far depths of space.

The four *Zôa* are the Lion, the Bull, the Man, and the Eagle. These symbols represent the four cardinal signs of the zodiac, constituting the so-called cross of the zodiac: Leo, Taurus, Aquarius (waterman), and Scorpio. The constellation Aquila, the Eagle, though extra-zodiacal, rising at the same time as Scorpio is frequently substituted for it. The word zodiac (*zôdiakos*) is derived from *zôdion*, "a little animal," a diminutive form of *zôon*, "an animal." Hence, the zodiacal signs being called *zodia,* the four principal ones are the *zôa.*

A scroll ("book") is the next symbol introduced. It is simply the human body, esoterically considered: it is "written *inside* and *at the back*," referring to the sympathetic and the cerebro-spinal systems, and "close sealed with seven seals," which seals are the seven major *chakras*. The sacrificial Lamb, the neophyte who has attained to the intuitive, noetic consciousness—which is symbolized by his having seven horns and seven eyes, that is, mental powers of action and perception—opens the seals (arouses the *chakras*) successively. As they are opened, however, they change to zodiacal signs, the zodiac being applied to the microcosm, man, as shown in the diagram here presented, the man being depicted as lying in a circle, and not standing upright as in the exoteric zodiac. The seven planets are assigned to the twelve signs of the zodiac in the order followed by Porphyrios, and, in fact, by all ancient and modern authorities. In Sanskrit works the planets are made to correspond also to the seven *chakras* in the following order, beginning with *mûlâdhâra:* Saturn, Jupiter, Mars, Venus, Mercury, Moon, and Sun. According to this zodiacal scheme, therefore, seven signs, with their planets, extend along the cerebro-spinal region, and correspond to the seven *chakras,* which are the focal centres of the *tattvas,* and have the same planets; while the remaining signs pertain to the five *prânas.*

When the Lamb opens one of the seals, one of the four *Zôa* thunders, "Come!" A white horse appears, its rider having a bow. This is Sagittarius, the Bowman or Archer. Iôannês thus starts the *kundalinî* current at the second *chakra,* and correctly so, for the *sushumnâ* does not energize until *îdâ* and *pingala* have reached the forehead, and then it starts from the first centre, corresponding to the terminus of the spinal cord. He therefore avoids calling this the first seal, but says, "one of the seals," and then numbers the others merely in the order in which they are opened.

The second seal being opened, the second *Zôon* says, "Come!" A red horse comes forth; to its rider is given a great sword, and power to take

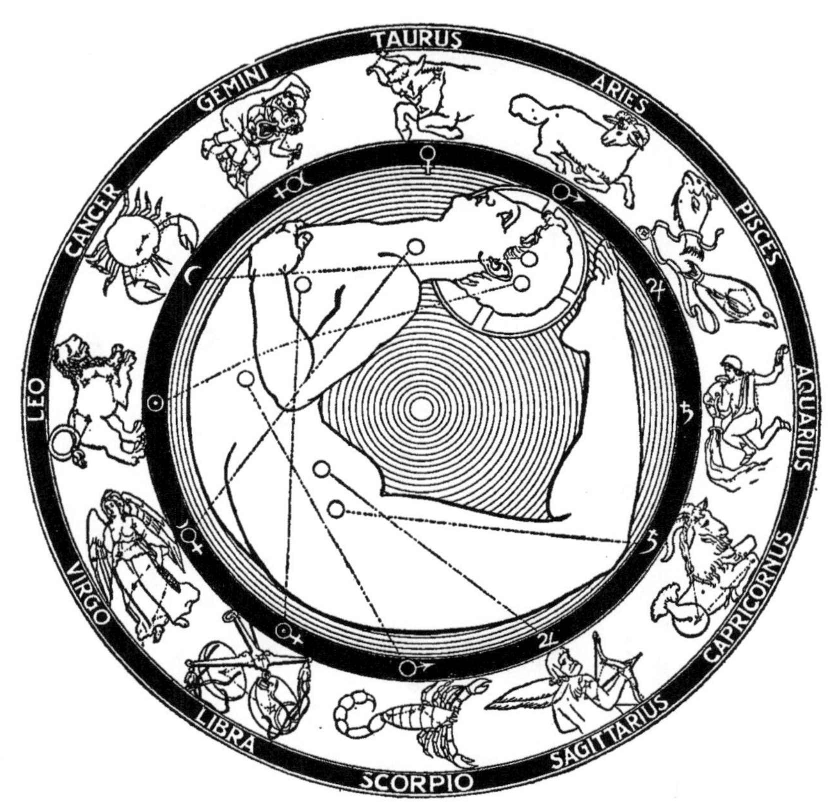

The Apocalyptic Zodiac

away peace from the earth. This is Scorpio, the house of Mars, the War-God.

Upon the opening of the third seal, the third *Zôon* says, "Come!" A black horse appears, its rider having a balance in his hand. This is Libra, the Balance.

When the fourth seal is opened, the fourth *Zôon* says, "Come!" A "pale" (*chlôros*, "yellowish") horse comes forth, and its rider is Death, accompanied by Hadês; they are given power over one quarter of the earth, to kill with sword, famine and death, and by the wild beasts of the earth. This is Virgo, the astrological sign of the womb. In the *New Testament*, as in the *Upanishads* and other mystical literature, "Death" is the name very frequently applied to the physical, generative world, in which birth, decay and death hold sway. In her character of the bad virgin, "a queen and not a widow," Virgo appears later in the Apocalyptic drama in the rôle of the Woman in scarlet, who is seated on the red Dragon, the epithumetic nature. But here she is associated with a higher centre which has to do with the psychic consciousness, and therefore Hadês, the psychic realm, is said to ride with Death; and the evil thoughts, desires and passions of the psycho-physical consciousness devastate the earth to the extent that they dominate.

The four horses, corresponding to the four *Zôa*, as also to the four beasts, are the four somatic divisions.

The fifth seal opened is the cavernous ganglion, to which corresponds the sign Cancer. Although Leo precedes Cancer in the zodiac, its corresponding *chakra,* the conarium, is the last of the centres to be aroused; for *îdâ* and *pingala* branch out to right and left at the forehead, and it is only the *sushumnâ,* starting at the sacral ganglion, that reaches the conarium. Yet the influence of the two currents, at this stage, causes a partial awakening of the lower centres in the brain; and this is stated by Iôannês in an ingenious little allegory about the uneasy ghosts ("souls") of those who had been sacrificed (atrophied, that is) because of the evidence they held. For it is by the atrophy of these noetic centres that man has lost the evidence of spiritual realities.

The sixth seal opened is the sacral plexus, to which corresponds the sign Capricorn. When this *chakra* is awakened, the *sushumnâ* passes along the spinal cord and impinges upon the brain. Words can not adequately describe the sensations of the neophyte upon his first experience of the effects produced by this mighty power: it is as if the earth crumbled instantly to nothingness, and sun, moon and stars were swept from the sky, so that he suddenly found himself to be but an unbodied soul alone in the black abyss of empty space, struggling against dread and terror unutterable. Thus Iôannês vividly pictures it, in terms of cosmic phenomena, as a seismic cataclysm, seemingly the end of the world. To the neophyte unprepared for this ordeal, failure may mean merely a short period of blank unconsciousness, or it may mean instant death—for this vital electricity has all the destructiveness, when misdirected, of the thunder-bolt. This sixth centre, *âjñâ,* is the great "lunar" *chakra,* where the currents bifurcate; and at this point the resurgent "solar" fires—those related to the cerebro-spinal system—form a cross in the brain. These solar forces Iôannês pictures as five Divinities, of whom four stand at the corners of the earth, presiding over the four winds, and a dominant Divinity, the fifth, who, bearing the signet-ring of the living God, ascends from the fifth direction of space, "the birthplace of the sun"—quite naturally, since he is in fact an aspect of that "Sun," the Nous. With his signet-ring he seals 144,000 out of the tribes of the children of Israel. The twelve tribes are simply the twelve zodiacal signs, symbolizing the twelve forces of the Logos, which differentiate into countless minor forces. These, in the microcosm, are the *nâdîs* of the *Upanishads*, which enumerate variously the *nâdîs* centring in the brain, but usually place the number at 75,000. Iôannês, however, holds to the zodiacal scheme: as each of the signs of the zodiac is subdivided into twelve minor signs, he multiplies these by 1,000—a number often used in mystical writings to express an indefinite term—and so arrives at a total of 144,000.

After this is seen a great multitude, from all nations and people of all languages, white-robed and pure, who wave palm-branches and sing a pæan before the throne; they are said to be those "coming out of the great ordeal." This "great ordeal" is reincarnation, the vast misery of being bound for ages to the wheel of birth. But this concourse of the "redeemed" who sing the chorus in this scene are the liberated elements in the aspirant's own nature; they are not a throng of people exterior to him. By evoking the marvellous potencies of his spiritual self-hood the Conqueror thereby regerminates all that was good, beautiful and true in each of his past incarnations, and so can say, in the magnificent language of the *Gospel of Phillip,* "I have united myself, assembling myself together from the four quarters of the universe, and joining together the members that were scattered abroad."

The seventh seal is the conarium, its zodiacal correspondence being Leo, which is the house of the Sun. Here reigns the Silence from which issue the seven spiritual "voices," or sounds. These mystic sounds Iôannês describes figuratively as trumpet-calls given successively by seven Divinities. They become audible when the *chakras* in the brain are awakened. The first four have a relation to the four somatic divisions, and react upon them; hence Iôannês ascribes to the trumpet-calls an obscuring or destructive effect upon the earth, the sea, the rivers and springs, and the sky, which correspond to the somatic divisions. At this stage of the telestic meditation the physical body is already in a state of trance, and it is now the lower psychic consciousness that is to be temporarily paralyzed or placed in abeyance; so, leaving the physical consciousness out of the reckoning, Iôannês terms the psychic the "third" as applied to each of the four planes, to which correspond the first four trumpet-calls. The results produced by the three remaining trumpet-calls he terms "woes," since they entail very trying ordeals, the issue of which is certain failure to the unpurified neophyte, of whom it has been said: "His vices will take shape and drag him down. His sins will raise their voices like as the jackals laugh and sob after the sun goes down; his thoughts become an army and bear him off a captive slave." Thus, at the fifth trumpet-call appears "a star fallen from the sky to the earth," who is the "Divinity of the abyss" and has the key to its crater, or opening, and whose name is *Apollyôn*, "he who utterly destroys," the "Murderer"; he opens the crater of the abyss, and from it emerges a locust-swarm of centaurs, who with their scorpion-like tails inflict torments on men. This "star" is Lucifer, the fallen "son of the morning," the *debased psychic mind of man*, which is indeed the ruler over the abysmal depths of desire, the bottomless pit of the passional nature, and the "murderer" truly of all that is pure, beautiful and true. This fifth trumpet-call refers to the carnal mind energizing in the sympathetic nervous system, the seat of the epithumetic consciousness, "the throne of the Beast"; and the next trumpet-call, the sixth, bears relation to the cerebro-spinal axis, the Apocalyptic "river Euphrates," and to what may be termed the psycho-religious consciousness, which manifests itself in the emotional worship of the unreal mental images of Deity—the lower phase of religion that indulges in irrational theologies, superstition, sorcery, fanaticism and persecution. The neophyte who has not thoroughly freed his mind from these pseudo-religious illusions will inevitably fail in the mystic meditation, which requires that all thought-images and preconceptions must be erased from the mind, so as to present it as a clean tablet for the inscription of truth. After this sixth trumpet-call, the four Divinities fettered at the river Euphrates are loosed: they are the solar regents of the seasons, ruling the quaternary divisions of the year, month, day and hour. The liberation of these forces is followed by the appearance upon the scene of an army of warriors mounted on lion-headed, serpent-tailed horses, who represent the countless powers of the Nous. A "strong" Divinity, the fifth, then descends from the sky, enveloped in a cloud, with a rainbow about his head; his face is luminous like the sun, and his feet resemble pillars of fire. This description of him is very similar to that of the Logos; he is, in fact, the Nous, for he and the four Euphratean Divinities are the analogues, on the purely intellectual plane, of the Logos and the four *Zôa*. The strong Divinity cries out with a lion-like roar, and seven thunders utter their voices. Concerning the utterances of these seven thunders Iôannês is very reticent. However, as the Greek language has but the one word (*phônê*) for both "voice" and "vowel," the meaning obviously is that the "great voice" of the Logos, who is the seven vowels in one, is echoed by the seven vowels, the sounds by which the higher forces are evoked; and these the seer is forbidden to write down. At this stage of the sacred trance the neophyte, having attained to the noetic consciousness, begins to receive the mystery-teachings, the "sacred, unspeakable words" (ἄῤῥητα ῥήματα) which, as Paulos says, it is not lawful for a man to disclose. When he shall have mastered the next noetic centre, the "third eye" of the seer, he shall pass beyond the illusions of time; "time shall be no more," and "the God-mystery shall be perfected." The Divinity gives a little scroll (booklet) to Iôannês, who eats it; and though honey-sweet in his mouth, it makes his belly bitter. The scroll symbolizes the esoteric instructions he has received, which are indeed bitter to the lower man, for they inculcate the utter extirpation of the epithumetic nature. He is then told that he must become a teacher, opposing the exoteric beliefs of the masses.

By a side-scene, a parenthetical explanation is given of the adytum or shrine of the God and the "two witnesses" of the "strong" Divinity, the Nous. The adytum—the temple-cell or fane in which the God is enthroned—is the seventh of the noetic centres; and the two witnesses are *îdâ* and *pingala*, the *sushumnâ* being the third witness, "the believable and true."

When the seventh trumpet-call is sounded, there is a choral announcement that the God, the true Self, has come to his own and will reign throughout the æons. The adytum is opened, disclosing the ark, the mystic receptacle in which were placed the "tablets" whereon was inscribed the contract of the God with man. Thereupon appears the Woman clothed with the Sun, star-crowned and standing on the moon; travailing, she gives birth to a man-child. She symbolizes the Light of the Logos, the World-Mother, that is, the pristine force-substance from which is moulded the solar body—her "man-child." The red Dragon, the epithumetic nature, seeks to devour her child; but it is caught up to the God's throne, and the Woman flees to the desert, where she is nourished three and a half years. This means that after the formation of the solar body has begun, any strong passion or emotion may disintegrate and destroy it; and that during the first half of the cycle of initiation (here placed at seven years) the nascent body remains in the spiritual world, as it were, while the *sushumnâ* force abides in its "place" in the material form, or "desert." For, strictly speaking, the solar body is not really born at this stage, but only has its inception. In the allegory, however, Iôannês could hardly employ the more accurate but less delicate mystery-representation of the Eleusinia.

Here the sacred trance ends for the present; and next follows a battle in the sky. The Dragon and his Divinities are hurled down from the sky by Mikael and his hosts; that is, the *mind* is now purified from the taint of impure thoughts. Mikael and his fellow Chief-Divinities (*archangeloi*), Uriel, Raphael and Gabriel, of whom he alone is named in the *Apocalypse*, are but the four *Zôa* in another guise. But the Dragon, though ejected from the intellectual nature, continues his persecutions on the lower plane.

The Beast, the phrênic nature, is described next. One of his seven heads (the seven dominant desires) has been slain, but comes to life; it represents the desire for sentient existence, the principle which causes the soul to reincarnate. This *will* to live, this passionate clinging to sensuous life, is expatiated on by Plato. Although the aspirant has apparently extirpated this longing, so far as the grosser affairs of the material world are concerned, it revives when he enters into the subtler planes of consciousness and perceives the psychic realms of existence. In Buddhistic literature it is termed *tanha* (the *trishna* of Sanskrit philosophical works); and in one ritual it is said: "Kill love of life; but if thou slayest *tanha*, take heed lest from the dead it rise again." Because this principle keeps man under the sway of reincarnation, Iôannês says significantly: "If any one welcomes captivity, into captivity he goes; if any one shall kill with the sword, with the sword must he be killed."

Another beast appears, who is the symbol of the generative principle. He participates in the nature of each of the other beasts, for he has two horns like the Lamb, talks like the Dragon, and has the magical powers of the Beast. He is called the Pseudo-Seer. His false seership is a certain very low form of psychism which, though not necessarily sensual, is due to the generative nervous ether. From this source come most of the "visions" of religious ecstatics, and the material manifestations produced by some spiritist-mediums; and, in a more general way, it is the source of the emotional element in exoteric religion, or so-called religious fervor, which is in reality but a subtle sort of eroticism. As a blind emotional impulse to worship, it stimulates the lower mind, the *phrên,* or Beast, to project an image of itself upon the mental screen and to worship that illusionary concept; and this—the "image of the Beast"—is the anthropomorphic God of exoteric religion.

Next appears again the Lamb, who by strict classification is one of the four beasts, though really too exalted to have that title applied to him, since he is the Nous, the regent of the highest of the four somatic divisions. With him are his many virginal attendants, who, as a prelude to the next act of the drama, chant a new pæan, to the accompaniment of many lyres. The neophyte has now become, as it were, like a lyre, with all the loose strings of his psychic nature tightened and tuned, tense and vibrant to the touch of his true Self.

The conquest of the cardiac centres is presented as a harvest scene, in which seven Divinities play their parts. Here, again, four of the septenate are related to the four somatic divisions. The fifth Divinity is "like the son of man," and with a sickle he reaps the "dried up" harvest of the earth. He is the Logos, or spiritual Self, which assimilates the higher aspirations and idealizing of the psychic nature—a harvest that is, usually, by no means abundant. The sixth Divinity, who comes out of the God's adytum, reaps the vine of the earth, and casts the ripe grapes into the great wine-vat of the God's ardor (*thumos*), and when the vat is trodden, *outside* the city, not wine but blood comes out, "up to the bridles of the horses, as far as 1,600 *stadia*." Now, while this sixth Divinity represents the Nous as intellect, the fifth Divinity reflects the aspect of the Logos as *Erôs*, or Divine Desire. The vine of the earth may be considered to be that vine of the purely human emotional nature, or feeling, whose tendrils are love, sympathy and devotion, and whose fruitage yields the wine of spiritual exaltation; but in the technical esoteric meaning the vine consists of the force-currents which correspond to the cerebro-spinal nervous system; while the great wine-vat of the God's ardor, outside the city (the physical body), is the auric ovum, which becomes suffused with an orange or golden color through the action of these currents in the cardiac centres. The horses are the four somatic divisions, and the number 1,600 is that of *to sôma hêliakon,* the solar body: the cardiac forces pervade and color the aura, imparting to it a golden hue, returning through the *chakras,* and circulating through the solar body—a process analogous to the nutrition of the fœtus, the solar body being, as it were, in a fœtal state. Thus the Woman is nourished in the desert, weaving for the soul its immortal and glorified robe.

It will be noticed that the word *thumos* is here rendered "ardor." The learned revisers of the "authorized" version translate it "wrath," making it a synonym of *orgê,* but changing to "fierceness" when, as in two instances, Iôannês has the two words so conjoined that the result of their theory, if carried out, would be the impossible expression "wrath of his wrath," which is, however, but little worse than one that is actually used, "the wrath of her fornication." But the word has not that meaning in the Platonic philosophy, or in that of the *Apocalypse,* which is practically identical with it. Plato makes *thumos* the energizing principle of the soul, intermediate between the rational nature (*to logistikon*) and the irrational (*to epithumêtikon*), and he explains that it is not a kind of desire, "for in the conflict of the soul *thumos* is arrayed on the side of the rational principle." It is a complex of emotions qualified by comprehensive ideas, as veracity, honor, pride, sympathy, affection, etc., and not at all an ordinary impulse of resentment. In Apocalyptic usage, *thumos* is likewise an energizing, creative principle; but whereas Plato, writing works of the more popular sort, confined himself to a threefold system and wrote with caution, Iôannês, using the medium of symbol and allegory, unintelligible to the profane, divulges the full fourfold system; he puts *phrên* as the intermediate principle between the psychic and the noetic nature, and elevates *thumos* to be the energizing principle of the latter. It thus corresponds to *Erôs,* the Divine Love, whose inverted reflection in the animal nature is *Erôs,* the love-god, or lust. With these two Erôtes of Grecian mythology he gives also its two Aphroditês, picturing them as the supernal virgin clothed with the sun and the infernal prostitute arrayed in scarlet, the two symbolizing respectively divine regeneration and human generation. Now, again, the word *orgê,* although signifying colloquially and in ordinary literature any violent passion, as anger and the like, has a more technical meaning in the terminology of the Mysteries, where it signifies the fecundating power or parturient energy in nature. The word is derived from *ὀργᾶν,* "to swell (with internal moisture)," as do plants and fruit from their sap, "to teem," "to swell (with passion)"; and from the same root comes *orgia,* the Mystery-rites practised in the worship of Iacchos, the phallic God.

Next follows the conquest of the generative centres. After a pæan chanted by the conquerors of the Beast, seven Divinities emerge from the adytum.

They are more majestic and more splendidly arrayed than the three septenates who have preceded them, and their part is to finish the regenerative work. One of the four *Zôa* gives them seven golden saucers (*phialai,* shallow libation-cups) containing the formative force of the Logos, "the *thumos* of the God." What ensues upon the outpouring of the creative potency is the eradication of the procreative centres—leaving thereafter but three somatic divisions—and the elimination from the other centres of every remaining vestige of psychic impurity. The first four Divinities act successively upon the four somatic divisions. The first Divinity pours out his saucer upon the earth, producing a painful sore on the men who had the brand of the Beast and worshipped his image. The force under the stimulus of which the lower psychic nature engendered pseudo-devotional illusions, irrational sentiments and emotions, and erroneous notions or concepts, now becomes the destroyer of these delusions, and of the psychic centres to which they are due.

The second Divinity pours out his saucer into the sea; it becomes as blood, and all creatures in it die. Every vestige of passion and desire is eliminated.

The third Divinity pours out his saucer into the rivers and springs, and they become blood. This is the somatic division of which the regent is the Beast, or phrênic mind, in which is centred the consciousness of the profane, the *polloi* who have persecuted and put to death many spiritual teachers and reformers. Here, again, Iôannês indulges in sarcasm; for he makes the Divinity of the waters (the Nous as presiding over this plane) say of the profane, "They poured out the blood of devotees and seers, and blood thou hast given them to drink, for they are *worthy*," a paronomastic use of the word *axios*, "deserving" and also "highly respectable." However, when the "blood of the Logos" suffuses the mystic centres of the heart "the knowledge from below" ceases to vaunt itself, and is replaced by "the wisdom from above."

The fourth Divinity pours out his saucer upon the sun, and it radiates scorching heat—alluding to the intense activity of the brain at this stage.

The fifth Divinity pours out his saucer upon the throne of the Beast, whose realm is thereby darkened, and whose subjects are afflicted with pains and sores. The Beast's throne is the great sympathetic nervous system, so that his realm extends over practically all the so-called involuntary physical and psychic functions; but, now that the four somatic divisions have been purified, the Beast is deposed, and henceforth the Nous is to reign supreme.

The sixth Divinity pours out his saucer upon the Euphrates, and its waters are dried up to prepare the path for the rulers who come from the source of the sun. These are the five "solar" Divinities who were erstwhile unfettered at the river Euphrates, the cerebro-spinal system. All the irredeemable elements of the man's lower self are now expelled, and they become a sort of entity external to him: as when, after the death of the physical body, all the evil psychic elements which are rejected by the soul before it enters the spiritual realm survive in the phantasmal world as a simulacrum, shade, or ghost of the dead personality, so upon the spiritual rebirth of a man—which connotes the death of his carnal nature, though the purified physical body continues to live out its allotted span—these expelled elements take shape in that same phantasmal world, or Tartarus, and remain there as a congeries of evil forces and impure elements, forming a malignant demon, which has no animating principle save hatred and lust, and is doomed to disintegrate in the cosmic elements. Thus Iôannês describes this gruesome thing in his allegory: he sees issuing from the mouths of the Dragon, the Beast and the Pseudo-Seer three unclean spirits, resembling frogs, who are "spirits of demons," and who collect all the evil forces and muster them for the last great battle upon the advent of the God.

The seventh Divinity pours out his saucer into the air (the aureola), and the enthroned God announces, "He has been born" (*gegone*). The authorized version gives the strained empirical translation, "It is done." But *genesthai* means "to be born," "to become," and is often used in the *New Testament* in the former sense, as in *Galatians* iv. 4, "born of woman." If used to convey the meaning "It is done," it would be dubious Greek; but here Iôannês is speaking quite openly of the new birth, whereas in his *Evangel*, where he depicts the new birth allegorically as the crucifixion, he gives the ultimate utterance as *tetelestai*, "It has been finished," referring to the initiation-rite, or "finishing" (*telos*), and conveying the esoteric meaning "He has initiated (perfected) himself." The spiritual birth is, in the Apocalyptic drama, accompanied by a general upheaval and readjustment: the great city, Babylon (the physical body), becomes three-divisional; the cities of the people (the procreative centres) are overthrown; and great hail (the condensation psychically of the auric substance) falls.

In the main action of the drama it is now that the Conqueror, the new-born Initiate, appears on his white horse; but the sequence of events is interrupted by a side-scene, which amounts to a parenthetical dissertation on the mysteries of physical existence and the epithumetic principle, symbolized by the Woman in scarlet and the fiery red Dragon. The Woman stands for Babylon, the physical body, and, in a more general sense, incarnate existence. She sits on the "many waters," the great psychic sea of sensuous life, and is likewise sitting on the Dragon—for he represents microcosmically the same principle that the sea does macrocosmically. The Dragon who sustains the Woman *was*, and *is not*, and yet *is;* for he is the glamour of sensuous life, the deceptive phenomena of which ever appear to be that which they are not. His seven heads are seven mountains where the Woman is sitting on them; that is, the seven cardinal desires energize through the seven *chakras* of the physical body during incarnation. It is then explained that there are seven rulers (kings), of whom five have perished, one *is*, and the other has not yet come, and when he comes he must abide a little while. The cycle of initiation extends through seven incarnations, which are not, however, necessarily consecutive; of these the Apocalyptic initiate is represented as having passed through five, and being now in the sixth; and in the seventh he will attain final emancipation. They are called kings because the only incarnations counted are those in which the aspirant is veritably the ruler of his lower faculties and propensities. The Dragon himself is an eighth, a sort of by-product of the seven, and he goes to destruction; for he is the phantom which forms after the final purification, and his fate is to disintegrate in the nether-world. His ten horns, or five pairs of horns, are the five *prânas*, each of which is both positive and negative. They are solar forces, the correspondences on the lowest plane of the Nous and the four *Zôa*, the regents of the four regions of space and the four divisions of time; but here, in the sphere of animal vitality, they energize the desires and passions. Thus they "have one purpose," and confer their power upon the Dragon, and rule with him each for one hour. They are the forces which in the innocent child produce its exuberant vitality and exquisite vivacity, but which in the individual who yields to the dictates of passion become wofully destructive; hence they are said to devour the flesh of the Woman in scarlet and consume her with fire.

Then comes a series of proclamations, exhortations and lamentations relating to the downfall of Babylon, the scarlet prostitute, who is the bad Virgo, the terrestrial Aphroditê, all of which applies to the complete subjugation of the physical body and its forces, and to liberation from the bondage of physical life. There are two "falls" in the allegory, paralleling the two crucifixions.

After this long but necessary digression, the action of the drama is resumed: the Conqueror appears, mounted on a white horse; "he treads the wine-vat of the ardor of the God's fecundating energy"; his mantle is blood-hued, and upon it and upon his thigh is inscribed his title of supreme ruler. The word "thigh" (*mêros*) is euphemistic; the *phallos, membrum virile,* is intended. This particular euphemism is common in the *Old Testament* (*Genesis* xxiv. 2, *et passim*). Moreover, it will be noticed that here the Conqueror has the sword of Mars, and is riding the white horse of the Archer who, at the opening of the first seal, the *adhishthâna chakra,* "came forth conquering and to keep on conquering." Thus the incarnated Logos is shown to bear a direct relation to the lowest centres. Now, it would be utterly impossible to elucidate the *Apocalypse* and ignore this delicate but perfectly pure subject, concerning which even the most communicative expositors of the esoteric philosophy have been extremely reticent; and so the present writer, being opposed to all undue secrecy, and believing that in this matter harm has resulted from the suppression of the truth, feels justified in dealing with the subject frankly and without constraint, though with necessary brevity. As every practical "pyrotechnist" knows, the human brain contains certain centres or components, including the pituitary body and the conarium, the higher functions of which are almost completely dormant in the normal individuals of the present races of mankind, who are therefore termed in the *New Testament* and other esoteric writings "the dead"; yet it is only through these organs of the brain that the spiritual Self of man, his overshadowing God, can act upon the consciousness of the psycho-intellectual self. This corpse-like condition of the finer organs of the brain does not preclude very high development of the ordinary intellectual faculties, apart from the epistemonic power; indeed, there are and always have been men who are lamentable examples of brilliant intellectuality combined with the densest spiritual stupidity. In the case of the true genius, the poet, artist, intuitive philosopher, and religious mystic of saintly purity, there is a partial awakening of these centres; while in the case of the seer (excluding from that class the mere psychic clairvoyant) the higher faculties are so quickened that he becomes cognisant of the interior worlds, the planes of true Being. But when the brain is fully restored to its true functions by the energizing of the *speirêma,* the *paraklêtos* of the *New Testament,* that "Light of the Logos" which is literally the *creative force of the Logos,* then it, the brain, becomes an androgynous organ, wherein takes place the immaculate conception and gestation of the self-born spiritual man, the *monogenês,* who is in very truth "born from above." This is the process of regeneration and redemption which Iôannês sets forth both in the *Apocalypse* and the fourth *Evangel,* and which Paulos and the three Synoptists have written in large characters easily to be read by him who has "the single eye," and which is expressed by myth and symbol in all the great world-religions of antiquity. There being a direct and intimate relationship and correspondence between the sacred centres in the brain and the lower procreative centres, it follows that true spirituality can be attained only when a pure and virtuous life is led; while for the neophyte who would enter upon the telestic labor, the task of giving birth to oneself, perfect celibacy is the first and absolute prerequisite. Unless he is inspired by the loftiest aspiration, guided by the noblest philosophy, and restrained by the most rigid moral discipline, his possibility of success is extremely remote; and the mere dabbler in the pseudo-occult will only degrade his intellect with the puerilities of psychism, become the prey of the evil influences of the phantasmal world, or ruin his soul by the foul practices of phallic sorcery—as thousands of misguided people are doing even in this age.

The Conqueror and his host are opposed by the Beast and his followers, and in the ensuing battle the Beast and the Pseudo-Seer are captured. They are thrown into the lake of sulphurous fire—which simply means that the rejected elements of man's animal nature return to the elemental kingdom whence they were derived—are thrown, as it were, into the great crucible of nature. The Dragon, however, is imprisoned for a thousand years, after which he must be let loose for a short time; that is, the Conqueror has yet one more incarnation to undergo, and therefore does not now destroy altogether the epithumetic principle, though in his next and final earth-life he will make short work of it. The thousand years, as a period between incarnations, merely express the apparent time on the spiritual plane, where, as Plato explains, sensation is of tenfold intensity, so that the thousand years, here as in the vision of Er, "answer to the hundred years that are reckoned as the life of man." The Dragon is disposed of, so far as the Apocalyptic drama is concerned; but Iôannês gives a paragraph in the future tense to tell of his final fate. But, finding it necessary to explain first, in a general way, what happens to the soul after death and between incarnations, he does so by describing a vision. He sees thrones and those seated on them, and judgment is passed on them. These represent a series of after-death judgments; for after each incarnation the incarnating Ego passes through a purifying ordeal or "judgment." All his activities during the past earth-life are reviewed; in the allegory they are described as souls revivified. Thus the souls of those that had been beheaded because they had the evidence of Iêsous (the Nous), and those who had not worshipped the Beast (that is, the latent intuitions that had been suffered to die in the mind, and the higher thoughts, emotions and aspirations) come to life and reign with the Christos (the Nous now illumined, *epistêmôn,* because freed from the body) for a thousand years, that is, during the non-incarnated period. But the rest of the dead (the thoughts and emotions that were concerned only with the carnal nature) do not come to life until the expiration of the celestial interregnum. They lie in latency until the Ego reincarnates, when they again become kinetic impulses. This coming to life of the nobler elements of man's nature, which were suppressed and slain during his earthly sojourn, is called "the first resurrection." Returning from this general exposition to the particular case of the Dragon in the drama (and hence changing to the future tense), Iôannês explains that this Adversary will be let loose at the expiration of the thousand years and will muster all the evil forces to make an assault on the beloved city—only to have his forces consumed by the divine fire, and himself be thrown into the lake of fire and sulphur, where the Beast and the Pseudo-Seer had already been sent, thus sharing with them the "second death."

But the physical body of the Conqueror is not dead; it is subjugated, purified and shorn of its passional centres. The downfall of Babylon expresses figuratively the death of the carnal nature; for in his regeneration the initiate has passed through a process analogous to death, and therefore he undergoes a judgment-ordeal similar to that meted out to the excarnated soul, but of vaster scope and mightier import. A great white throne appears, and from the face of the enthroned Majesty the earth and the sky flee and vanish, for he is the perfected Self of the Man, higher than earth and heaven, greater than all the Gods. He is summing up the cycle of his incarnations, and on all the elemental forces and faculties of his composite nature which have made up his many personalities of the past he renders judgment "according to their works." All these, "the dead" in the three lower worlds, spring to life and are "judged," as Iôannês reiterates, "every one according to their works." The condemned elements of the physical and psychic natures ("Death and the Unseen") are thrown into the lake of fire, the chaotic "eighth sphere" in which the creative fire refines, as material for future æons, the hylic refuse of each cycle; and this is termed the "second death."

Then appear a new sky and a new earth, that is, the subjective and the objective consciousness of the Nous on its own plane; but the sea, the sensuous consciousness of the lower plane, has passed out of existence. The holy city, the deathless solar body, now comes down out of the sky, enveloped in its halo, or radiance (*hê doxa*), the sun-robe of the God. This aureola is self-luminous, with an opalescent glitter; it is the "wall" of the city, having twelve gateways (the orifices of the body), and at the gateways twelve Divinities (the twelve great Gods of the Zodiac, or cosmic forces), and with the names of the twelve tribes of Israel (the zodiacal signs) inscribed on the gates; the tribes are in four triads, assigned to the four regions of space. The wall of the city has twelve foundations, which have on them the names of the twelve apostles of the Lamb; these are the twelve powers of the Logos, the spiritual archetypes of the twelve cosmic forces; for in symbology the "foundation" of all things is in spirit, upon which rests the structure of whatever is manifested. The measurements of the city and its wall have already been explained, together with the enigma of its cubical form; the further details relating to it will be elucidated in their proper place in the commentary.

"*Aum.* Come thou, O Thought Divine! The grace of the Divine Thought be with the holy devotees. *Aum.*" Thus ends the *Apocalypse* of Iôannês, one of the most stupendous allegories ever penned by the hand of man.

So comprehensive, complete and coherent is the *Apocalypse,* that its full beauty, even in its fine finish of details, can be perceived only when it is viewed as a whole; nor can its deeper meaning be grasped by mere analytical study. Its multiplicity of details and reduplication of symbols have utterly baffled all attempts to analyze it by empirical methods; and the exotericists have fared even worse through inability to distinguish from the main action of the drama the explanatory matter introduced by means of side-scenes. Yet, in reality, the construction of the drama is not complicated, and its characters are not numerous. Its *dramatis personæ* are:

- △. The God, the for ever concealed DIVINE PRESENCE.
- I. The First Logos (*logos endiathetos*, immanent idea), the DIVINE LOVE, from whom proceed:
- II. (a) The Second Logos (*logos prophorikos*, uttered thought), the DIVINE THOUGHT, the ruler of the cosmic forces; symbolized by the Conqueror, the Sun;
  (b) The Light of the Logos, Archê, the DIVINE SUBSTANCE, primordial matter; symbolized by the Sky-Virgin, the Moon. As Philo Judæus says (*De Confus. Ling*, p. 267) the Logos is the Archê; as Spirit-Matter they are one in essence. They emanate:

III. The Twelve Powers, of which five are noetic (solar) and seven are substantive (lunar); symbolized by the Twelve Zodiacal Constellations. The twelve powers, emanated successively on four planes of existence, make forty-eight cosmic forces; and, with Archê-Logos, forty-nine.

These are the sole performers in the Apocalyptic drama, though some of them assume various rôles. The ancient zodiac was subdivided into sections of ten degrees each, called decans, giving three to each of the twelve signs; and to each of these thirty-six subdivisions was assigned an extra-zodiacal constellation, a paranatellon, which rises or sets simultaneously with it. These forty-eight constellations, twelve in the zodiac and three sets of twelve beyond it, with the Sun considered as the centre and making up the number forty-nine, completed the stellar scheme of the zodiac, which is faithfully adhered to in the *Apocalypse*. The seven sacred planets play their parts in the drama; but they only represent seven aspects of the Sun. The extra-zodiacal constellations Draco, Cetus, Medusa and Crater are especially prominent as characters in the drama. The First Logos takes no active part, and is but a voice speaking from the throne.

The *dramatis personæ* and scenic arrangement are shown in the diagram on page 68.

It should be borne in mind, however, that these are the worlds and forces of the microcosm, man, as portrayed in the zodiacal scheme; and, as the two triangles represent the conflicting spiritual and ani-

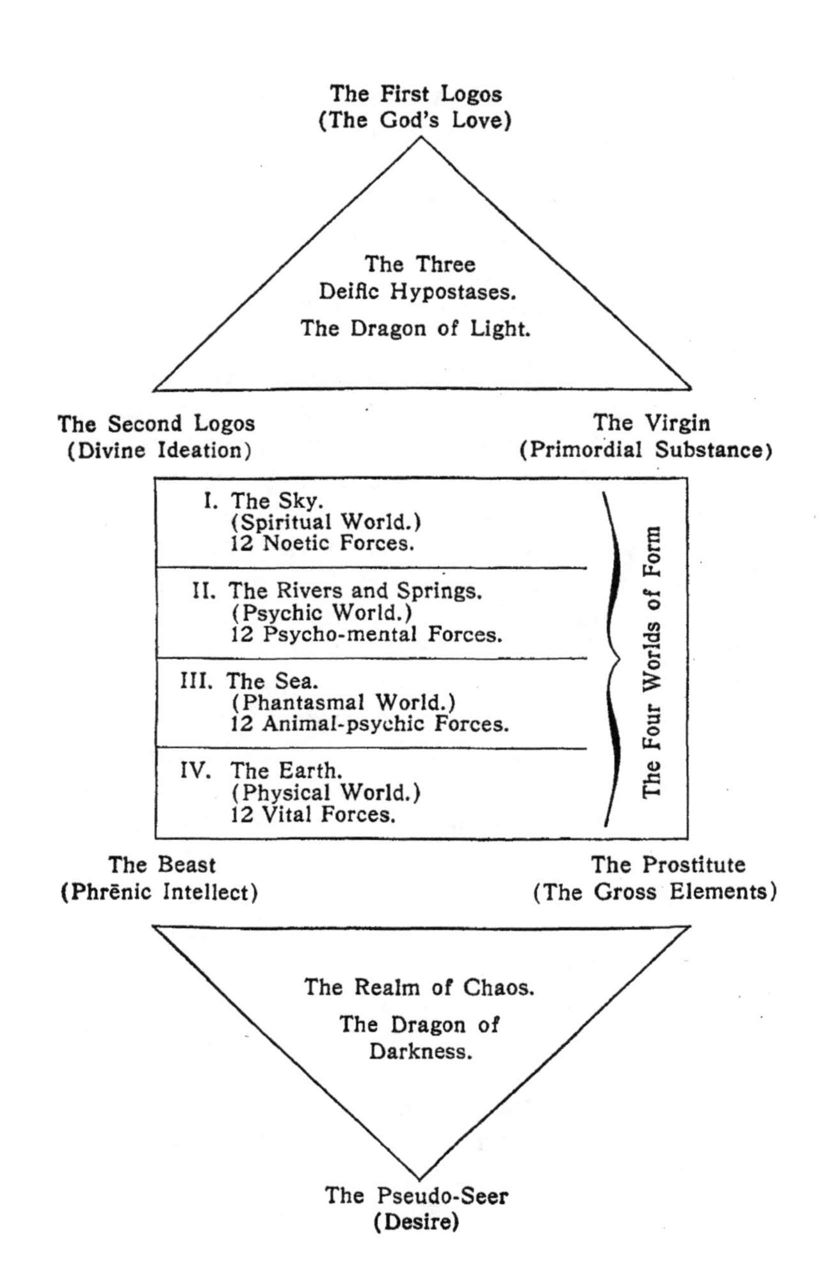
The First Logos
(The God's Love)
The Three
Deific Hypostases.
The Dragon of Light.
The Second Logos
(Divine Ideation)
The Virgin
(Primordial Substance)
I. The Sky.
(Spiritual World.)
12 Noetic Forces.
II. The Rivers and Springs.
(Psychic World.)
12 Psycho-mental Forces.
III. The Sea.
(Phantasmal World.)
12 Animal-psychic Forces.
IV. The Earth.
(Physical World.)
12 Vital Forces.
The Four Worlds of Form
The Beast
(Phrēnic Intellect)
The Prostitute
(The Gross Elements)
The Realm of Chaos.
The Dragon of
Darkness.
The Pseudo-Seer
(Desire)

mal principles in the human soul, they should be considered as being interlaced in man, the "perfect square," and enclosed within the auric *plêrôma*, or divine synthesis, thus:

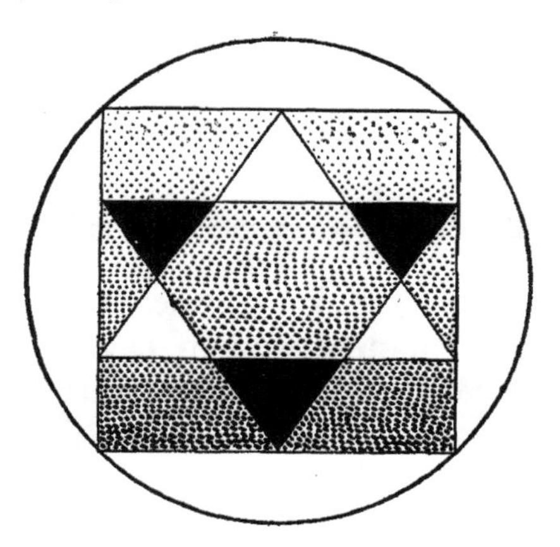

The four planes of existence are represented in the *Apocalypse* as (1) the Sky, (2) the Rivers and Springs, (3) the Sea and (4) the Earth; while encompassing these four is the Air, the Empyrean, which is called the fifth world in the Ptolemaic system, although it really stands for the three formless planes.

The twelve forces energizing on each of the four manifested planes, or worlds of form, are divided into a five and a seven; the five is subdivided into a one and a four; and the seven is subdivided into a three and a four, the three being subdivided into a one and a two. These divisions, written diagrammatically as if on a measuring-stick, make the "rod" with which to "measure the adytum of the God, the altar, and those who worship in it," excluding "the court which is exterior to the adytum"—the lower triad:

<table>
<tr><td rowspan="2">1</td><td colspan="4" rowspan="2">4</td><td>1</td><td colspan="2">2</td><td colspan="4" rowspan="2">4</td></tr>
<tr><td colspan="3">3</td></tr>
<tr><td colspan="5">5</td><td colspan="7">7</td></tr>
<tr><td>1</td><td>2</td><td>3</td><td>4</td><td>5</td><td>6</td><td>7</td><td>8</td><td>9</td><td>10</td><td>11</td><td>12</td></tr>
</table>

This "measuring-stick" applies to each of the four manifested planes; and in each of them the fivefold group relates to the Sun and the Rectors of the Four Regions of Space, symbolizing variously the Logos and his four manifested powers, the Nous and the four intellective faculties, etc.; and the sevenfold group relates to the Moon and her septenary time-periods.

The fivefold group, which is really a quaternary and a dominating power, in each case corresponding to the Archê-Logos, is shown, with a few of its many correspondences, in the table on facing page.

The drama has seven acts: (1) the opening of the seven seals, the conquest of the seven principal centres of the sympathetic nervous system; (2) the sounding of the seven trumpets, the conquest of the seven centres of the brain, or cerebro-spinal system; (3) the battle in the sky, resulting in the expulsion of the Dragon and his Divinities, that is, the elimination from the mind of all impure thoughts; (4) the harvesting of the earth and its vine, the conquest of the seven cardiac centres; (5) the outpouring of the seven scourges, the conquest

Δ	Worlds	Archetypes	Principles	Forces	Somatic Divisions	Elements and Senses
	Empyrean. Aura.	Logos. Eagle.	Nous.	The Conqueror.	White Horse.	Æther. Touch.
I.	Sky. Spiritual World.	Bull. Taurus.	Lamb. Aries.	7 Divinities of the Trumpet-calls.	Dun Horse. Head.	Air. Hearing.
II.	Rivers and Springs. Psychic World.	Lion. Leo.	Leopard-Beast. Leopardus.	7 Divinities of the Harvest.	Black Horse. Heart.	Fire. Sight.
III.	Sea. Phantasmal World.	Man. Aquarius.	Dragon. Draco.	7 Divinities of the Seals.	Red Horse. Abdomen.	Water. Taste.
IV.	Earth. Physical World.	[Scorpion.] Scorpio.	Pseudo-Seer. Medusa.	7 Divinities of the Scourges.	White Horse. Procreative Centres.	Earth. Smell.

of the generative centres, which finishes the "conquest of the *chakras*" and brings about the birth of the solar body; (6) the battle in the psychic world, or infernal region, called "Harmagedôn," resulting in the overthrow of the three beasts, that is, the extinction of the extraneous phantasmal demon, or composite elemental self; and (7) the last judgment, the summing-up of the completed cycle of earth-lives. All the remaining portions of the book are explanatory and descriptive. Of these seven acts, four (the conquests of the *chakras*) relate to the four somatic divisions, and the other three to the mental, psychic and auric principles. Tabulated, the four acts that are concerned with the conquest of the centres, in their bearing upon the process of regeneration, are as shown on page 73.

In a general way, the four conquests made by the Logos-Sun correspond to the four seasons of the year: the opening of the seals, the beginning of man's spiritual resurrection, is Spring, the time of germinating seed, expanding bud and upspringing vegetation; the energizing of the noetic centres, the trumpet-calls awakening to life the sunlike intellectual faculties, is Summer, the season of sturdy growth and hastening to ripeness, the over-fervid sun at times scorching the tender-green growth; the opening of the heart-centres, the harvesting of the earth and the vine, is Autumn, the period for gathering and garnering the fruitage; and the conquest of the lower life-centres, the scourging of all that is base and impure in man's nature, is Winter, the season of purifying frost and cold, which prevail until the returning Sun, lengthening the days, is

Correspon- dences	The Old Universe	Act I 7 Seals	Act II 7 Trumpet-calls	Act III 7 Harvesters	Act IV 7 Scourges	The New Universe
1. Creative Centres.	The Earth.	Archer on White Horse.	The third of the Earth's vegetation burnt up.	Æonian Tid- ings to those dwelling on the Earth.	Libation poured into the Earth.	A New Earth.
2. Psychic Centres.	The Sea.	Swordsman on Red Horse.	The third of the creatures in the Sea destroyed.	Fall of Babylon announced to those who drank her wine.	Libation poured into the Sea.	No more Sea.
3. Phrēnic Centres.	The Rivers and Springs.	Weigher on Black Horse.	The third of the Rivers and Springs become wormwood.	Denunciation of those who worship the Beast's Image.	Libation poured into the Rivers and Springs.	No more Sorrow.
4. Noetic Centres.	The Sky.	Death and Hadēs on Dun Horse.	The third of the Sun, Moon and Stars darkened.	Solar Divinity appears, hav- ing a Sickle.	Libation poured upon the Sun.	A New Sky.
5. Sympathetic System.	The Abyss.	Souls of the Dead under the Altar.	The Crater of the Abyss opened.	The "over- ripe" Harvest is gathered.	Libation poured upon the Throne of the Beast.	The dual Tree of Life.
6. Cerebro-spinal System.	The River Euphratēs.	Five Divinities of the five directions of Space.	Five Divinities of the River Euphratēs.	The Vine is Reaped.	Libation poured upon the River Euphratēs.	The River of Life.
7. The Aura.	The Air.	The Silence.	The Virgin.	The Winepress.	Libation poured into the Air.	The "Glory." (Aura.)

mystically reborn as the Christ-child, the Sun-God of a new divine year, the æon of the deified man.

Thus, it will be seen, the Apocalyptic drama is expressed in terms of natural phenomena: its hero is the Sun, its heroine the Moon; and all its other characters are Planets, Stars and Constellations; while its stage-setting comprises the Sky, the Earth, the Rivers and the Sea. It elucidates its subject with the glare of lightning, proclaims it with the roll of thunder, emphasizes it with the shock of the earthquake, and reiterates it with the Ocean's voice, the ceaseless murmur of its "many waters." Ever it maintains this cosmic language, this vast phrasing of nature. In the first magnificent chorus of Constellations who encircle the throne of the Sun-God the starry hosts praise him as the creator of the universe; yet when the drama has been enacted that universe has perished, "the first sky and the first earth are passed away, and the sea exists no more." Then from his effulgent throne the Logos-Sun announces, "Behold! I am making a new Universe." Now, this Apocalyptic Universe is Man, the lesser cosmos, of whom the Logos-Sun is in truth the Architect and Builder, and whom the Sun, the Moon, and all the Stars of heaven have helped to mould and make: for in every human creature, however fallen and degraded, are stored up all the forces, both cosmic and deific, which brought him into existence and have nurtured him throughout the vast cycle of generation, in countless incarnations upon earth, while the Logos of Light has taught him the loving lessons of the Good, the Beautiful and the True, and the Logos of Darkness has held before him the dread lessons of the Evil, the Ugly and the False; and these same creative forces of the Light-giving Logos, with the tireless patience of the deathless Gods, but await the time when the resurgent divine life again stirs within him, and then, disintegrating the elements composing the carnal man, they begin a new evolution, the work of "making perfect" this child of the æons, whom the Sun-Adversary, "the Scorpion-monster of Darkness," can drag down till he is lower than the beasts, but whom the Logos-Sun, the Eagle of Light, can exalt above the Gods.

Ἐγώ εἰμι τὸ φῶς τοῦ κόσμου· ὁ ἀκολουθῶν μοι οὐ μὴ περιπατήσῃ ἐν τῇ σκοτίᾳ, ἀλλ᾽ ἕξει τὸ φῶς τῆς ζωῆς.

The Light of the World am I; he who goes along with me shall not at all walk about in the darkness, but shall have the light of the [supernal] life.

Jn. viii. 12.

THE INITIATION OF IÔANNÊS

The white hair of hoary

Κρόνος Ω

(Saturn)

The blazing eyes of wide-seeing

Ζεύς Υ

(Jupiter)

The keen sword of

Ἄρης Ο

(Mars)

The shining face of

Ἥλιος Ι

(Sun)

The chitōn and girdle of

Ἀφροδίτη Η

(Venus)

The swift feet of

Ἑρμῆς Ε

(Mercury)

The wave-murmuring voice of

Σελήνη Α

(Moon)

Τὸ Φῶς τοῦ Κόσμου

(The Light of the Cosmos)

THE INITIATION OF IÔANNÊS

CHAPTER I. 1, 2

The initiation of Anointed Iêsous, which the God conferred on him to make known to his slaves the [perfections] which must be attained speedily. He sent his Divinity and by him symbolized [them] to his slave Iôannês, who gave evidence of the Logos of the God and of the evidence of Anointed Iêsous—of all the [visions] that he saw.

COMMENTARY

In the Greek Mysteries, which were also called the "perfecting" or "finishing" rites, the candidates for initiation, after receiving some preparatory training in semi-exoteric lesser rites, were termed *mystai*, "veiled ones," while the Initiates were called *epoptai*, "those having super-sight"—or seers. The word *apokalypsis*, "unveiling," is clearly a substitute for *epopteia*, "initiation into seership." That Iôannês could not possibly have intended the title of his occult treatise to convey the meaning of "revelation" is evident from the nature of the work, which is not only profoundly esoteric and couched in the mystery-language of the zodiac, but also has its meaning so impregnably intrenched behind symbolism, allegory, anagram, number-words, and other puzzling devices, that it has successfully withstood the assaults of "those without" (the exotericists) for nearly two millenniums. Its sub-title also, by the word "symbolized" (*esêmanen*), likewise indicates that it was not written as light literature for the profane. True, the "authorized" translators render the verb "signified"; yet with bland inconsistency they ascribe the sense of "miracle" to the substantive *sêmeion*, which properly means a "symbol," or a "sign," as a constellation or sign of the zodiac.

The title makes Iôannês the one to be initiated (unless it is taken as merely indicating his authorship, which in the light of the text is hardly a reasonable supposition), while the sub-title gives Iêsous as the candidate for initiation who emerges as the Conqueror after the telestic ordeals; for here, as in the fourth *Evangel*, Iôannês and Iêsous are but one individuality, Iôannês representing the incarnated man, and Iêsous his noetic Self, whose "slave" the material man truly must become if he wills to reach the heights celestial. The Divinity who comes at the behest of Iêsous is higher than Iêsous himself; for he is the Logos, who in the initial vision makes his appearance as the "son of man," and remains throughout as the Hierophant, or Initiator, while Iêsous is the candidate who is subjected to the initiatory trials and has to do the perfecting "works," whereby he finally becomes the Conqueror on the white horse—the new Initiate in his solar body. The spiritual perfections have to be attained "speedily" by sustained, unremitting effort; yet, as time is regarded by those who look upon earth-life as an affair of but one incarnation, the telestic work would seem by no means expeditious; for it requires not less than seven incarnations of untiring effort before the final goal is reached. But the "path" of the esotericist is indeed a short-cut, and his a speedy journey, as compared with the progress of those who are content to follow the common highway of evolution, and who will reach their divine destination, their promised land, only after long ages of aimless wandering in the wilderness of terrestrial life.

It is the intuitive mind—"Anointed Iêsous"—that gives evidence of the Logos to the neophyte, and he in turn must, according to the law of the occult, transmit it to his fellow-men—who usually repay him with some form of physical or mental martyrdom.

CH. I. 3

Immortal is he who discerns, and they who learn [from him], the arcane doctrines of this Teaching, and observe the [precepts] which are written in it; for [their] season is near.

COMMENTARY

This is a dedication of the book to every mystic who may succeed in penetrating to its inner meaning, and impart to other students the occult doctrines (*logoi*) it contains. For the "Logoi (oracles) of the Lord" are esoteric aphorisms having in them the potency of the Divine Thought, and are not mere "words" comprehensible to the conventionalist. Likewise, *prophêteia* is not merely "prophecy" in the fortune-telling sense of predicting future events; the word means literally "speaking for" (the Gods); the office of the seer being to receive and interpret the truths taught in the noetic world, the realm of the Logos. The writings of Ezekiel, Zechariah, and the other Hebrew "prophets," are esoteric treatises on the nature of man, thinly disguised as predictions. In them, nations and personages play the parts that in the *Apocalypse* are acted by the heavenly bodies.

The word *makarios* means much more than simply "blessed." It connotes the state of the immortal Gods (emancipated souls), as expressed by the Sanskrit term *sachchidânanda,* "true being, consciousness and bliss." To the man or woman who resolutely pursues the path of purity and devotion, there will come unfailingly this consciousness of immortality and spiritual calm; it is but a matter of centring the mind upon the deathless inner Self instead of upon the outer self that is under the sway of alternating death and birth. This mental reverting is the *metanoia* of the *New Testament,* not merely "repentance," but "changing the mind" from the mortal to the immortal mode of thought.

CH. I. 4, 5

Iôannês to the seven Societies which are in Asia: Grace to you, and peace, from [the enthroned

God] who [for ever] *is*, who was, and who is coming, and from the seven Breaths that are before his throne, and from Anointed Iêsous, that believable witness, the first-born from "the dead," and the foremost of the rulers of the earth.

COMMENTARY

The word *ekklêsia,* meaning an assembly, or group of people called together for some special purpose, a society, applies very neatly in the allegory to a nervous plexus, or ganglion, which consists of nucleated cells acting as a centre of nerve-force to the fibres connected with it. The seven Societies are the seven principal ganglia; later they are metamorphosed into "seven little lampstands," each ganglion being a little brain, a minor light-giver in the body, as the brain is the great light-giver, or microcosmic sun; and then they are changed almost directly into "seven seals" on a scroll, the *chakras* being indeed sealed in the materialistic person, so far as concerns their psychic functions.

The enthroned God is the First Logos, who abides in the Eternal, and is not to be considered as incarnated, but rather as overshadowing the man on earth. The word "coming" (*erchomenos*) is used because the future participle of the verb "to be" (*esomenos*) would convey an erroneous metaphysical concept; "was," in the imperfect tense, expresses an action still continuing, but the future, "shall be," would imply something that does not yet exist, whereas the Logos is represented as subsisting in an infinite Present which includes in itself the Past and the Future. In his *Evangel* (viii. 58) Iôannês expresses the same idea by the words, "Before Abraham was born, I *am*." Thus also Plato teaches (*Timaios*, 38) that it is erroneous to attribute the past and the future to the Eternal; "For we say, indeed, that he was, he is and he will be; but 'he is' alone approximates the true concept (*logos*); for 'was' and 'will be' are properly to be said only of generation in time."

The two Logoi are practically one, the distinction between them being purely metaphysical.

The seven Breaths (*pneumata*), which appear later as seven stars (the seven planets), are the Chief-Divinities, Mikael, Gabriel, etc., representing seven aspects of the Logos. Iêsous Christos, the first-born from "the dead," is the epistemonic (intuitive) Mind; the intuition is the first of man's dormant spiritual faculties to awaken, bringing certainty of knowledge, and becoming the dominant power in his life.

The pronoun "y o u," plural, in this translation is thin-spaced, to distinguish it from "you" in the singular.

CH. I. 5, 6

To him who, having graciously welcomed us and washed us from our sins in his blood, also made us rulers and sacrificers to his God and Father—to him be the glory and the dominion throughout the æons of the æons! AMÊN.

COMMENTARY

These words of Iôannês refer to the initiation he has passed through, and which he is about to describe. The lustration (*baptismos*) of blood, which emancipates from sin, is the rain of purifying fire (the "blood" of the Logos) poured out by the Divinities charged with the seven scourges. By a bold oriental simile, a variant of the parable of the prodigal, the higher Self is represented as hospitably entertaining the returned wanderer, the reincarnating self, and washing from him the stains of travel.

To each of the planets a distinctive attribute is assigned; and here "dominion" applies to the Sun. and "glory" to the Moon.

The *Amên* is the Greek equivalent of the Sanskrit *Aum,* the latter being pronounced with a nasal prolongation, called *ardha-mâtrî,* "half measure," thus giving the Apocalyptic "time, [two] times and half a time." Used in a certain way, this word has the power, through the correlation of sound and the vital electricity, to arouse the *speirêma,* or regenerative force. To use it effectively, one must know not only its correct pronunciation but also the predominant color and the key-note of his own aura.

CH. I. 7

Behold! He comes amidst the clouds, and every eye shall see him, and they who pierced him [shall see him]; and all the tribes of the earth shall wail over him. Verily! AMÊN.

COMMENTARY

The eyes that see him are the noetic centres; they who "pierced him" are the sense-perceptions; and the "tribes" are the repentant elements of the mental and psychic constitution. The "clouds" are the auric forces; here the nimbus seems to be referred to rather than the aureola; the latter envelopes the entire body, while the nimbus is limited to the head. In conventional Christian art the nimbus of the "Father" (who is, in fact, the First Logos and *not* the Supreme Deity) is represented of a triangular shape, irradiating light-rays; that of the Crucified (the Second Logos) contains a cross; and that of the Virgin (Archê) has a circlet of stars. In the Christos-mythos there are *two crucifixions,* corresponding respectively to generation and to regeneration. The first crucifixion is the descent of the soul into matter, when the physical body becomes its "cross" and the five senses are its five "wounds"; the human figure, with extended arms, forming a cross, and the objective senses being avenues that lead away from the spirit. The second crucifixion is the ascent of the soul to spirit through the initiation-rite, or self-conquest, when it is mystically said to be crucified in the brain—in the *place* called *Golgotha,* "the skull."

CH. I. 8

"I am the Alpha and the Ô," says the Master, the God who [for ever] *is,* who was, and who is coming, the All-Dominator.

COMMENTARY

In apposition to the announcement of the coming of the Crucified, the uncrucified First Logos, the Eternal, declares, "I am the Α and the Ω," which formula includes the five intermediate vowels, Ε, Η, Ι, Ο and Υ, and is equivalent to saying, "I am the seven vowels in one." Cedrenus says (p. 169) that the Chaldæans symbolized the Light of Reason (*noêsis*) by the vowels α ω. These two vowels, the first and the last letters of the Greek alphabet, were assigned to the Moon and Saturn, the intermediate planets answering to the five other vowels in their order. Thus Achilles Tatius (*Isagog.*, p. 136) correctly ascribes the seven vowels to the planets as follows: Α, Moon; Ε, Mercury; Η, Venus; Ι, Sun; Ο, Mars; Υ, Jupiter; and Ω, Saturn. The seven Planetary Powers are potential in the First Logos; in the Second Logos they become manifested potencies. The title "All-Dominator" is solar; *Hêlios pantokratôr* dominates all the planets, and the title is applicable to either Logos. The revised version retains the anachronistic "Omega," a word coined in the middle ages to designate the letter Ω.

CH. I. 9–11

I, Iôannês, who am your brother, as also your copartner in the ordeal, ruling and patience of Iêsous, came to be in the island which is called Patmos, through the arcane doctrine of the God and through the evidence of Iêsous. I came to be in the Breath[-trance] on the master-day, and I heard behind me a loud voice, like a trumpet-call, saying:

"What you see, write in a scroll, and send [the message] to the seven Societies which are in Asia: to Ephesos, Smyrna, Pergamos, Thyateira, Sardeis, Philadelpheia and Laodikeia."

COMMENTARY

Serene patience is one of the indispensable qualifications of the aspirant for spiritual knowledge, and so is the "ruling," or dominance of the higher intellect, the Nous (Iêsous), over the lower faculties. The ordeal (*thlipsis*) is that of initiation, now begun. Through the awakening noetic perception (the "evidence of Iêsous") and the increasing light from the Logos—the whitening of the dawn of the new life—the aspirant becomes isolated, and in the drear loneliness of one who has for ever abandoned the illusions of sensuous existence, but has not yet seen the sunrise of the spirit, he dwells, as it were, on an island, apart from his fellow-men. Then through his introspection comes the message of the Great Breath, and in the sacred trance he attains his first *autopsia*, beholding the apparition of his own Logos.

CH. I. 12–16

I turned about to see the Voice which was speaking with me. Having turned, I saw seven little golden lampstands, and in the midst of the little lampstands an [apparition] like the son of man, wearing [a vesture] reaching to the feet and girded at the paps with a golden girdle. His head and his hair were white as white wool, [white] as snow; and his eyes were as a blaze of fire. His feet were like the liquid-metal that is as if it had been melted in a furnace. His voice was as the voice of many waters. In his right hand he had seven stars. From his mouth kept flashing forth a keen two-edged sword. His face was [luminous], as shines the sun by its inherent force.

COMMENTARY

This apparition is a fanciful picture of the Sun as the *Panaugeia*, or fount of all-radiating light; and like all the puzzles of Iôannês it is ingeniously constructed. The "voice" that speaks is the primary aspect of the Second Logos, in whom the seven "voices" or vowels (for *phônê* is the one Greek word for both "vowel" and "voice") become differentiated. As the all-pervading solar Light he walks about among the seven golden lampstands, the seven planetary bodies, holding in his right hand their seven "stars," the light which he confers upon them. The Logos-figure described is a composite picture of the seven sacred planets: he has the snowy-white hair of Kronos ("Father Time"), the blazing eyes of "wide-seeing" Zeus, the sword of Arês, the shining face of Hêlios, and the *chitôn* and girdle of Aphroditê; his feet are of mercury, the metal sacred to Hermês, and his voice is like the murmur of the ocean's waves (the "many waters"), alluding to Selênê, the Moon-Goddess of the four seasons and of the waters. To have placed the winged feet of Hermês on the figure, or to have used the ordinary word *hydrargyros* ("water-silver") for mercury, would have made the puzzle altogether too transparent; so Iôannês has employed the archaic word *chalkolibanon*, which he evidently borrowed from Plato, to designate the material used in fabricating the feet of his Planetary Logos. Plato speaks of *chalkolibanon* (*Kritias*, p. 114) as a metal mined by the Atlantians and esteemed by them as the most precious of metals except gold—which it is, in the series of esoteric correspondences. He does not describe it, but says, "*Chalkolibanon* is now only a name, but was then something more than a name," a statement that is no more than a sarcastic comment on the spiritual degeneracy of the times. But in his highly technical alchemical work, the *Timaios* (p. 59), he unmistakably describes this metal, calling it simply *chalkos* and ranking it as a primary metal next to gold, as "a sort of bright and condensed fluid." The word is rendered "fine brass" in the authorized version, although brass was unknown to the Greeks, who used a bronze composed of copper and tin. But *chalkos* was used as a general term for metal, as well as for copper in particular; and *chalkolibanon* is simply the "metal that forms in drops," as does gum exuding from a tree. It is neither "brass" nor "incense-gum," but simply quicksilver—fluidic, "as if melted in a furnace."

This figure of the Sun as the ruler of the planets is a symbol of the incarnated Self, the Second Logos; and, as given in the description of the apparition, the seven planets are in reversed order, for the Second Logos is the *inverted reflection* of the First: the celestial man is, as it were, upside-down when incarnated in the material world. The significance of this inversion develops later in the Apocalyptic drama.

Similar descriptions of the "son of man" are to be found in *Ezekiel, Zechariah* and *Daniel,* but though similar they are not the same; for the *Apocalypse* is *sui generis*, and while Iôannês *apparently* borrows many symbols and poetic images from the ancient writings, he usually employs them to cloak his real meaning by endowing them with a different or a variant significance. Hence the exotericists who attempt to follow these supposed parallels will only be misled and confused, as Iôannês doubtless intended they should be; and, since this commentary is not concerned with the esotericism of the Hebrew writings, the usual references to them will be omitted. The real parallels between the *Apocalypse* and Plato's writings are much more numerous and striking than these deceptive ones that are to be found in the Hebrew scriptures.

CH. I. 17–20

When I saw him, I fell at his feet as one dead. He placed his right hand on me, saying:

"Be not afraid. *I* am the First [Adam] and the Last [Adam], he who is Alive. I became a 'dead man'; and, Behold! I am alive throughout the æons of the æons, and I have the keys of Death and of the Unseen. Write down the [glories] you saw, also those which *are,* and those which are about to be attained next after them, [beginning with] the mystery of the seven stars which you saw on my right hand, and the seven little golden lampstands. The seven stars are the Divinities of the seven Societies; and the seven little lampstands are the seven Societies.

COMMENTARY

The esoteric tenet as to "the First and the Last" is very clearly stated by Paulos (I *Cor.* XV. 22, 45): "For even as in the Adam[-man] all became moribund, so likewise in the Christ[-man] all are restored to life." "The first man, Adam, was born in a living psychic form (*psychê*), the last Adam in a life-producing breath (*pneuma*)."

The Logos, or Divine Man, becomes "dead" during the long cycle of material evolution; but as it emerges from material conditions through the awakening of the epistemonic faculty, or spiritual intuition, it is restored to life; for the man has then the consciousness of immortality, and holds the keys with which he can unlock the prison-doors of the physical world ("Death") and the psychic world, or Hadês, the "Unseen." This representation of incarnated life as the death-like obscuration of the soul is very common in ancient mystical literature. Plato puts forward the idea repeatedly, as in the punning etymology of the *Kratylos* (p. 400): "Some say that the body (*sôma*) is the tomb (*sêma*) of the soul, which may be considered as buried in our present life."

The cities of the seven Societies were on the

The Seven Cities in Asia

mainland, not far from Patmos. Starting with Ephesos, the nearest to the island, they extended in a circular form, and thus answered admirably the purpose of the allegory. But that there was no Christian Society at Thyateira history is positive, and is somewhat dubious about the others. Ephesos was celebrated for her wonderful temple of Diana, the Huntress Goddess, whom the Romans connected with the sign Sagittarius; and Sardeis had a temple to the Goddess Rhea, the "Mother," who was quite the moral reverse of the chaste Diana. At Pepuza, a desert place in Phrygia not far from Patmos and the seven cities, there was a centre of the Mithriac Mysteries.

A marked peculiarity of the *Apocalypse* and the fourth *Evangel* is the constant use of diminutive forms, as "little lampstands"; for in both works Iôannês deals with the microcosm. The small lampstands are the *chakras*, and their "stars" are the differentiated forces of the *speirêma.*

CHAPTER II. 1–7

"To the Divinity of the Society in Ephesos write:

"These [words] says he who with his right hand dominates the seven stars, he who walks about in the midst of the seven little golden lampstands: I know your works, and your over-toil and patience, and that you can not bear wicked men. You put to the test those pretending to be apostles (and they are not!) and found them false. You endured and have patience; on account of my name you have toiled and have not grown weary. But I have [this complaint] against you, that you left your first love. Remember, therefore, whence you are fallen; reform, and do the first works—but if not, coming to you speedily, I shall move your lampstand out of its place, unless you do reform. But you have this [virtue], that you abhor the works of the Nikolaitanes, which I also abhor. He who has an ear, let him hear what the Breath is saying to the Societies.

"THE CONQUEROR—to him I shall award to eat [the fruit] of the tree of life which is in the middle of the Garden of the God.

COMMENTARY

To this Society the Logos announces himself in his aspect as MEMORY, the faculty of receiving and retaining impressions, which links together the past, present and future, and is thus the power upon which depends the continuity of the individual consciousness. The ever-toiling and unwearied memory stores up all the experiences of the individual, throughout the long cycle of incarnations, and no memories are ever lost save those that are evil and therefore suffer the "second death" after the final purification of the soul.

Kronos

The *mûlâdhâra chakra* (represented by Ephesos) lies at the base of the spinal cord, and being thus at the lower pole of the cerebro-spinal system, and the starting-point of the *sushumnâ*, it is directly related to the highest, the *sahasrâra*, or conarium; for, as already explained, the lower plane of life is the inverted reflection of the higher. Hence it is said to have left its first love (the divine love having become human love), and is told to remember whence it has fallen and do the first works —that is, pour its force into the first and highest *chakra*, the regenerative brain-centre. The quality of this *chakra* still retains somewhat of the higher love, a clinging to purity and an aversion to sensuality and every perversion of the creative function. It is therefore said to have exposed the impure charlatans and to abhor the works (secret rites) of the Nikolaitanes. The latter were a pseudo-occult sect who practised the vilest forms of phallic sorcery. The unclean worship of the "Great Mother," called Rhea, Cybele, Astartê, and by other names, was wide-spread in Asia, and many were her temples, with their "consecrated women." But in the older mythology Rhea was not thus degraded.

The attainment of spiritual knowledge is in effect the process of reviving the memory of the incarnating Ego in relation to the supernal worlds, before it became immured in matter; and this memory of things divine can be recalled only through the action of the *paraklêtos*, the regenerative force. Hence in this aspect the Nous is said to hold in its grasp the seven stars and to walk about among the seven little lampstands. According to Plato, all true knowledge is derived from the "recollection of the things in which the God abides": the immature souls, who can not "feed on the vision of truth," fail of being "initiated into the mysteries of Being, and are nourished with the food of opinion," but "he who employs aright these memories is ever being initiated into the perfect mysteries, and alone becomes perfect."

As the sun enters each sign of the zodiac it is said, astrologically, to "conquer" the sign and to assimilate its particular quality; and the same is said of the *kundalinî* as it passes through the *chakras*. Hence the hero of the *Apocalypse*, who is the Nous, or microcosmic Sun, is called "the Conqueror."

The award to the Conqueror, in the aspect here presented, is the Eternal Memory: he shall eat the fruit of the tree of life (the fruitage of the life-cycle) in the God's own abiding-place, the mystical Paradise, or state of ineffable bliss.

In this aspect the Logos is Kronos (Saturn), the God of Time; the corresponding vowel is Ω, and the quality ἰσχύς, "strength," the power of holding and retaining.

CH. II. 8–11

"To the Divinity of the Society in Smyrna write:

"These [words] says the First [Adam] and the Last [Adam], who became a 'dead man,' and came to life: I know your ordeal and poverty (but you are rich!) and the profanity of those claiming to be Ioudaians—and they are not, but are an assembly of the Adversary. Do not fear the [ordeals] which you are about to undergo. Behold! The Accuser is about to cast some of you into prison, that you may be brought to trial; and you will have an ordeal of ten days. Become confiding until death and I shall give you the crown of life. He who has an ear, let him hear what the Breath is saying to the Societies.

"THE CONQUEROR shall not at all be punished by the second death.

COMMENTARY

Here the Logos is presented in his aspect as REASON, the highest philosophical intellection (*noêsis*), which in the carnal man is dormant, but which awakens when he turns to the serious consideration of the concerns of the higher life.

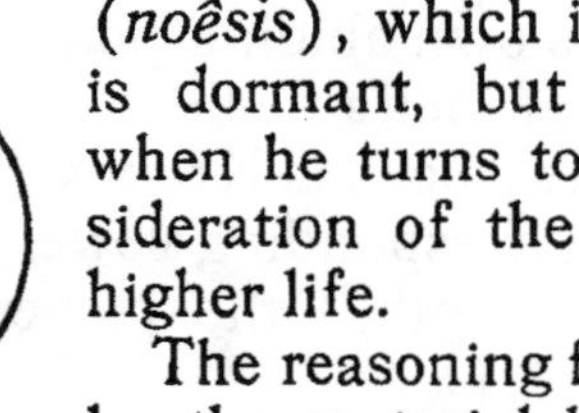
Zeus

The reasoning faculty, hampered by the material brain, is poverty-stricken; but when freed from the trammels of matter it is rich in ideas. The pseudo-Ioudaians are the irrational dogmas of exoteric religion, which are put forth as divine revelations, though they are obviously opposed to reason, and are but the mere vagaries of the phrênic mind when under the stimulus of the perverted devotional nature, and come, therefore, not from the Logos but from his adversary, Satanas, the foe of intellectual light. The Hebrew language was at first a secret sacerdotal jargon of Egyptian origin, and St. Gregory of Nyssa asserts (*Oratio*, p. 12) that the most learned men of his day knew positively that it was not as ancient as other languages and did not become the spoken language of the Jews until after their departure from Egypt. The word "Jew" is used throughout the *Apocalypse* in its Kabalistic meaning, for one having esoteric knowledge, an initiate; as in the Kabalistic maxim, "The stone becomes a plant, the plant an animal, the animal a man, the man a Jew, and the Jew a God." Hence came the myth of the "chosen people."

The "ten days" refer to a zodiacal decan and a paranatellon—here, the constellation Draco, the "archaic snake," who is the prosecutor or accuser, the theological "Devil" and "Satan."

This *chakra*, the *adhishthâna*, is the starting-point of *îdâ* and *pingala*, which are allegorized in the *Apocalypse* as the "two witnesses," the *sushumnâ* being the third.

The reward of the Conqueror is Conscious Immortality: he is to wear the crown of life, and nothing that originates in the spiritual mind shall pass into the oblivion of the second death.

This aspect of the Logos is that of Zeus (Jupiter), the son of Kronos and the father of Gods and men, who was also called *Zeus Triôpês*, the "Three-eyed," and was represented on the Acropolis of Argos by a gigantic statue having two eyes in its face and one on the top of its forehead. The corresponding vowel is Υ, and the attribute *σοφία*, "skill."

CH. II. 12–17

"To the Divinity of the Society in Pergamos write:

"These [words] says he who has the keen two-edged sword: I know your works, and where you dwell—where the throne of the Adversary is. You are holding fast my name, and you did not abjure belief in me even in the days in which [the oracle was] Antipas, my believable witness, who was slain among you, where the Adversary dwells. But I have a few [complaints] against you, because you have there those who uphold the teaching of Balaam, who taught Balak to set a snare before the children of Israel, to eat [food] offered to ghosts, and to prostitute. So, also, *you* have those who uphold the teachings of the Nikolaitanes, which I abhor. Reform—but if not, coming to you speedily, I shall combat them with the sword of my mouth. He who has an ear, let him hear what the Breath is saying to the Societies.

"THE CONQUEROR—to him I shall award to eat a share of the occult manna; and I shall award to him a white voting-pebble, and on the voting-pebble [will be] a new name engraved, which no one knows but he who receives it.

COMMENTARY

To this Society the Logos presents himself in his aspect as WILL, volition, the energizing principle, and he carries, therefore, the sword of the War-God.

Pergamos stands for the *manipuraka chakra,* the solar plexus, which is the chief centre of the sympathetic nervous system, and the seat of the epithumetic nature—the Dragon, or Satanas, the Adversary of the Logos. Plato states (*Timaios*, p. 70 *et seq.*) that the desires are "chained down like a wild beast" in the region between the midriff and the navel, "and knowing that this principle in man would not listen to reason" and "was liable to be led away by ghosts and phantoms of the night and also by day, the God, considering this, formed the liver, to connect with the lower nature and to dwell there, contriving that it should be compact, smooth and bright, and both sweet and bitter, in order that in it the energy of the thoughts, proceeding from the mind (*nous*), might be received like figures in a mirror and projected as images." Thus, he says, the creative powers, in order that the lower nature "might obtain a measure of truth, placed in the liver their oracle (*to manteion*)—which is a sufficient proof that the God has given second-sight (*mantikên*) to the foolishness of man." "Such then, is the nature of the liver, such its function and place, as said, formed for the sake of second-sight." This, of course, is the faculty of the *mantis*, or individual gifted with "second-sight"; and this is also the "witness Antipas," who has indeed been slain by those who have lost even this psychic function of the liver, as well as the intuition of the intellectual nature. ANTI-ΠA-Σ is simply MANTIΣ disguised by having its initial M converted into ΠA (*pa*) and anagrammatically transposed. To solve the puzzle, it is only necessary to combine the letters Π and A, forming IAI, which when inverted

Arês

makes a passable M— and incidentally shows why "eminent scholars" have failed to find a satisfactory Greek derivation for the word or any historical record of the supposed "martyr."

The snare of Balak, the eating of food devoted to spirits, and sexual promiscuity, all refer to various goêtic practices, the nature of which is best left unexplained.

The reward to the Conqueror, who by the dauntless energy of the will vanquishes all the evil foes in his own nature and fights his way to the pure region of spiritual light, is that he has imparted to him the secret knowledge, the Gnôsis, and is given, as it were, a ballot, being named and naturalized a citizen of the republic of the initiated.

Here the Logos has the semblance of Arês (Mars). The corresponding vowel is O, and the attribute δύναμις, "force."

CH. II. 18–29

"To the Divinity of the Society in Thyateira write:

"These [words] says the son of the God, who has his eyes as a blaze of fire and his feet like the liquid metal: I know your works, and your love, belief, service and patience; and that your last works [are to be] greater than the first ones. But I have [a complaint] against you, that you tolerate the woman Iezabêl, who, professing to be a seeress, teaches and deludes my slaves to prostitute and to eat [food] offered to ghosts. I gave her time, that she might reform; but she does not will to reform from her prostitutions. Behold! I throw her down on a [sick-]bed, and those committing adultery with her [I shall subject] to a grievous ordeal, unless they shall reform from their works. I shall slay her children in the Death[-world]; and all the Societies shall know that *I* am he who searches into kidneys and hearts. I shall give [awards] to each of y o u according to your works. But to y o u I say, to the rest in Thyateira—as many as do not possess this teaching, who remained guileless of knowledge concerning the depths of the Adversary, as they say—I do not cast on y o u an additional burden. Nevertheless, that which y o u do possess, retain dominion over it till I come.

"THE CONQUEROR—who also observes my works until the perfecting-period—to him I shall award authority over the people, and he will rule them with an iron wand (like vessels of clay they are being crushed!) as *I* also received [authority] from my father. And I shall award to him the morning star. He who has an ear, let him hear what the Breath is saying to the Societies.

COMMENTARY

To this centre the Logos presents himself in his aspect as DIRECT COGNITION, the faculty of apprehending truth without the aid of inductive reasoning; and in this aspect as the Sun, the pure intellectual effulgence, he is not the "son of man," but is the "son of the God," having the all-seeing eyes of Zeus and the winged feet of Hermês, thus combining the attributes of the Divine Reason and the Divine Thought.

Hêlios

Thyateira represents the *anâhata chakra*, the cardiac centre. As the liver, the organ of divination, is the reflector of the mind in the epithumetic region, so the heart is the organ which in the phrênic region serves as the reflector of the Nous, and is therefore the centre of the higher psychic consciousness. The corresponding reflector in the brain is the conarium; and the generative organs, the "three witnesses," or inverted analogue of the higher triad, fulfil the same psychic function in the lowest of the four somatic divisions; hence the allusion to the "kidneys" or "loins"—an euphemism for *testes*. The four virtues enumerated, love, belief, service and patience, correspond to the four noetic qualities as transmitted through the heart.

The pseudo-seeress Iezabêl has the name and attributes of the sorceress, Ahab's wife, of malodorous memory, in the *Old Testament* story. She here represents the emotional, erotic sort of psychism which is sometimes developed at orgiastic "religious revivals," and which is more characteristic of hysterical women than of rational human beings. By this prostitution of mind and emotion to the base epithumetic nature, causing moral disintegration and the dissipation of psychic energy, mediumistic faculties are sometimes developed, opening up avenues of communication with the shades of the dead, the disgusting larvæ to whom the misguided medium quite literally offers as food the elements of his own disintegrating personality.

The award to the Conqueror—if he also heeds the works of the Logos, that is, observes the admonitions of the spiritual mind—is the absolute dominion over the lower faculties and forces, which he rules as with a rod of iron; and he receives the morning star, which symbolizes the Divine Love that heralds the coming day of full spiritual illumination.

Here the Logos has the aspect of Hêlios (the Sun); the corresponding vowel is I, and the attributes, three in number, are *κράτος*, "dominion," *πλοῦτος*, "wealth," and *εὐχαριστία*, "thanks" or "all-graciousness," the latter epithet implying that the Sun-Logos unites in himself all the graces, or good qualities, of the seven planets.

CHAPTER III. 1–6

"To the Divinity of the Society in Sardeis write:

"These [words] says he who has the seven Breaths of the God and the seven stars: I know your works: that you have the name that you are alive, but that you are a dead man. Become awakened [from the dead] and strengthen the remaining [affections] that are on the point of dying; for I have not found your works accomplished before my God. Therefore, remember how you have received [this message] and heard [it]; and observe [its precepts], and reform. If, therefore, you will not be awake, I shall come upon you [silently] as a thief [comes], and you will not at all know what hour I shall come upon you. But you have a few names in Sardeis who did not sully their garments, and they shall walk with me in white [raiment], for they are deserving.

"THE CONQUEROR—he shall thus be clothed in white garments, and I shall not at all erase his name from the book of life, but I shall acknowledge his name before my Father and before his Divinities. He who has an ear, let him hear what the Breath is saying to the Societies.

COMMENTARY

To this Society the Logos proclaims himself in his aspect as the DIVINE LOVE, the deific creative energy; and here he is the synthesis of the seven planets (stars) and the seven creative forces (*pneumata*), thus corresponding, in a way, to the First Logos, or Erôs.

Aphroditê

Sardeis represents the *vishuddhi chakra*, the centre in the throat, which is directly related to the lower creative centres, as is shown by the change of voice at the time of puberty and the castrato voice of the eunuch.

The throat is also peculiarly affected by the finer emotions.

This higher love is here said to have the name of being alive, yet to be dead in reality; for the devotional aspirations and purer affections of humanity are indeed pitifully weak and moribund. It is this deadness of the moral feelings that stills the voice of conscience; yet at any time that conscience may unexpectedly speak out, bringing remorse and sorrow to him whom the Self has thus suddenly aroused, coming upon him silently, like a thief in the night. This simile is repeated in xvi. 15, with almost the same wording.

The city of Sardeis was a centre of Venus-worship, having a temple of Astartê.

The reward to the Conqueror is perfect purity; and the auric color corresponding to this *chakra* (its esoteric "name") will remain in the aureola (the book of life), or "glory"; emotion becoming transmuted into the eternal gladness.

In this aspect the Logos is Aphroditê (Venus), the Goddess of Love; it is only in this female aspect that the Logos is the creative "Word" (in one sense the occult potency of sound), and therefore identical with Vâch, "speech," who is also Sarasvatî (Venus) in Hindu mythology. The corresponding vowel is H, and the attributes are εὐλογία, "invocation," and βασιλεία, "realm," or "ruling."

CH. III: 7–13

"To the Divinity of the Society in Philadelpheia write:

"These [words] says he who is Holy, who is True, who has David's key, who opens and no one shall shut, who shuts and no one opens: Behold! I have swung open before you a door which no one can shut. For [I know] that you have a little force; and you observed my arcane doctrine, and did not abjure my name. Behold! I am giving [deliverance to some of you] from among the assembly of the Adversary [composed] of those professing to be Ioudaians—and they are not, but are lying. Behold! I shall cause them to come and make obeisance before your feet, and to know that *I* have graciously received you. Because you guarded the arcane doctrine of my patience, *I* also shall guard *you* from the [first] hour of that probation which is about to come upon the entire homeland, to put to the proof those who are dwelling upon the earth. Behold! I am coming speedily. Retain a firm grasp on the [steadfast virtue] which you possess, so that no one may carry off your crown.

"THE CONQUEROR—I shall make him a pillar in the adytum of my God, and never more shall he go outside of it; and I shall write on him the name of my God, and the name of the city of my God, the new Hierousalêm, which is coming down out of the sky from my God; and [I shall write on him] my new name. He who has an ear, let him hear what the Breath is saying to the Societies.

COMMENTARY

Here the Logos presents the aspect of the DIVINE THOUGHT, the pure and unmixed nature of intellect, or the unrefracted light of the Nous—Thought not differentiated into thoughts, but considered as the energizing principle of Mind, and the complement of the energizing principle of Love. "The Holy" and "the True" are identical with "the Good" and "the True" of Plato, while the correlated Aphroditê-aspect is "the Beautiful."

Hermês

According to Kabalistic mysticism, ADaM stands for Adam, David and Messias, making the Messias the reincarnation of Adam and of David: these represent three stages in man's life-cycle, Adam being the primeval state of childlike innocence, David the adolescence in which good and evil struggle for the mastery, and Iêsous (Messias) the stage of spiritual maturity. David, for all his vileness and evil deeds, had the virile depth of feeling, philosophic breadth of mind and poetic insight that give promise of the spiritual man; and these were his "key" to the door giving entrance to the spiritual consciousness. Compare with this xxii. 16 and commentary.

Philadelpheia stands for the *âjñâ chakra,* the centre at the forehead. This centre is the point of divergence of the auric light, the color of which reveals infallibly the spiritual status of each individual. Thus, if the light radiating from it is golden-yellow, it is the "name" of the Sun; if dull red or green, it is the "brand of the Beast."

The reward of the Conqueror is that he is to become a sustaining power in the spiritual world, no more to reincarnate, but to abide in the eternal city, the solar body.

The aspect of the Logos here is that of Hermês (Mercury), the God of Occult Wisdom. The corresponding vowel is E, and the attributes are τιμή "honor," and σωτηρία, "deliverance."

CH. III. 14–22

"To the Divinity of the Society in Laodikeia write:

"These [words] says the AMÊN, the witness believable and true, the origin of the God's organic world: I know your works, that you are neither cold nor hot. I would that you were cold or hot! So, because you are lukewarm, neither hot nor cold, I am on the point of vomiting you from my mouth. Because you say, 'I am rich, I have become rich, and *I* have lack of nothing,' and do not know that *you* are the worn-out, pitiable, beggarly, blind and naked one, I advise you to buy from me gold tried by fire—so that you may be rich—and white garments—so that you may clothe yourself, and the shame of your nakedness not be apparent—and eyesalve to anoint your eyes—so that you may see. As many as *I* love, I confute and instruct. Therefore be emulous and reform. Behold! I am standing at the door and gently tapping. If any one hears my voice and opens the door, I shall visit him; and I shall dine with him, and he with me.

"THE CONQUEROR—I shall award to him to be seated with me on my throne, as *I* also conquered and was seated with my father on his throne. He who has an ear, let him hear what the Breath is saying to the Societies."

COMMENTARY

To this Society the Logos announces himself as the DIVINE SUBSTANCE, Archê, from which originate all the elements, both subtile and gross, including those forms of matter which the modern physicist classifies as "forces."

Selênê

Laodikeia represents the *sahasrâra chakra,* the atrophied "unpaired eye." Hence the allusion to the Phrygian "eyesalve."

Neither cold nor hot, that is, having neither the dispassionate reason nor the devotional fervor, but lukewarm and nauseating to the spiritual mind, the lower mind yet prides itself on its supposed wealth of intellectual attainments; yet, without the gold of spiritual refinement and the white garments of purity, these attainments are meagre and unlovely.

The reward of the Conqueror is to share the throne of the God, to become one with his own highest Self.

Here the Logos has the semblance of Selênê (the Moon), the "white-armed" Goddess who rules the four seasons and the waters. The corresponding vowel is A; and the attributes are δόξα, "glory," and ἐξουσία, "authority."

Tabulated, with their correspondences, the seven aspects of the Logos are as follows:

Societies and Centres	Planets and Vowels		Aspects	Attributes	Rewards to Conqueror
Ephesos. Sacral.	♄	Ω	Memory.	Strength.	Continuity of Consciousness. (Tree of Life.)
Smyrna. Prostatic.	♃	Υ	Reason.	Skill.	True Being. (Crown of Life.)
Pergamos. Epigastric.	♂	O	Will.	Force.	Spiritual Power and Knowledge. (Occult Manna and Voting-pebble.)
Thyateira. Cardiac.	☉	I	Direct Cognition.	Dominion. Wealth. Thanks.	Dominion over All Faculties. (Iron Wand.)
Sardeis. Pharyngeal.	♀	H	Divine Love.	Praise. Ruling.	Eternal Bliss. (Book of Life.)
Philadelpheia. Cavernous.	☿	E	Divine Thought.	Honor. Deliverance.	Emancipation from Reincarnation. (Pillar of Adytum.)
Laodikeia. Conarium.	☽	A	Divine Substance.	Glory. Authority.	The Solar Body. (Throne of the God.)

In the seven benedictions contained in the *Apocalypse* twelve attributes are given; of these three are assigned to the sun, two to each of the members of the higher triad, and one to each of the lower.

When the two triads (the sun being always the central planet) are paralleled, the result is a fourfold system, in which the Christos-faculty, *epistêmê*, stands alone, and the other faculties are paired, as shown in the following table:

	PLANETS	FACULTIES	ATTRIBUTES
1.	Hēlios (Sun).	Direct Cognition.	Dominion. Wealth. Thanks.
2.	Arēs (Mars). Aphroditē (Venus).	Will. Love.	Force. Praise. Ruling.
3.	Zeus (Jupiter). Hermēs (Mercury).	Reason. Thought.	Skill. Honor. Deliverance.
4.	Kronos (Saturn). Selēnē (Moon).	Memory. Substance.	Strength. Glory. Authority.

CHAPTER IV. 1–3

After these [things] I saw; and, Behold! a door opened in the sky; and it was that first voice which I [now] heard, like a trumpet-call speaking to me, [the enthroned God] saying:

"Come up hither, and I shall make known to you the [perfections] which must be attained hereafter."

Immediately I came to be in the Breath[-trance]. Behold! a throne was placed in the sky, and on the throne [a God] was seated. The enthroned [God] was in appearance like an opal and a carnelian, and a rainbow encircled the throne, in appearance like an aqua-marine.

COMMENTARY

This trumpet-like voice is that of the First Logos, the Enthroned Eternal (ch. i. 8), and not that of the Planetary Logos who sent the messages to the seven Societies.

The names of the precious stones in the Greek are somewhat uncertain; but here it is obvious from the context that the ἴασπις was what is now called the opal, and the σμάραγδος the aqua-marine, or blue beryl.

The somatic divisions in the *Apocalypse* agree with the symbolism of the Jewish tabernacle, except that the latter was semi-exoteric, following the threefold system. Thus Josephus says of the tabernacle and its arrangements: "They represent in some sort the universe. For out of the three portions into which the length of the tabernacle is divided, the two into which the sacrificing priests are allowed to enter represent the Earth and the Sea, which are open to everyone, and the third portion, which is inaccessible to them, is like the Sky, which is reserved for God, because it is his dwelling-place."

CH. IV. 4–8

Encircling the throne were twenty-four thrones, and on the thrones [I saw] twenty-four Ancients seated, arrayed in white garments, and [wearing] on their heads golden crowns. From the throne went out lightnings, thunders and voices; and [there were] seven lamps of fire burning before the throne, which are the seven Breaths of the God. Before the throne [was a sheen] as a glassy sea, like crystal. In the middle of the throne and in a circle about the throne [were] four Beings, full of eyes before and behind. The first Being was like a Lion; the second Being was like a young Bull; the third Being had the face of a Man; and the fourth Being was like a flying Eagle. The four Beings, having each one of them six wings, are full of eyes round about and within; and ceaselessly day and night they keep saying:

"Holy, holy, holy [is] the Master-God, the All-Dominator, who *was*, who [for ever] *is*, and who is coming!"

COMMENTARY

The four Beings, or four operative Powers of the Logos, correspond to the four great planes of existence and, therefore, also to the four *manteias*, or states of seership, on each of those planes. (When Iôannês speaks of being "in the Breath" he uses the word *pneuma* in place of *manteia*, "trance," as the latter word would be too explicit for allegorical purposes.) Each of these four states of seership has a subjective and an objective phase on the plane to which it relates; and this is symbolized by the many exterior and interior eyes of the Beings. As already explained, the Nous has its "reflector" in each of the four somatic divisions. As macrocosmic powers, the four Beings are mystically the four quarters of the zodiac, the four arms, so to say, of the sun; and as solar forces each is a septenate, radiating from a focal point into the six directions of space. Similarly, the time-periods are divided into fourths, as the year, which has four seasons, each containing three months, these being again subdivided into bright and dark fortnights, making twenty-four such periods, corresponding to the twenty-four hours of the day. The forces which, whether in the macrocosm or the microcosm, govern successively these various time-periods are the twenty-four "very old men" (*presbyteroi*), the Ancients, and they are identical with the twenty-four wings of the four Beings.

The glassy sea is the ether specialized in the brain; the aura of the *chakras* being represented by the seven fire-lamps or Breaths.

CH. IV. 9–11

And as often as the Beings gave glory, honor and thanks to the [God] seated on the throne, to him who lives throughout the æons of the æons, the twenty-four Ancients kept falling down [successively] in front of the [God] seated on the throne, worshipping him who lives throughout the æons of the æons, and letting fall their crowns in front of the throne, saying:

"Worthy thou art, our Master and our God, to receive the glory, the honor and the force; for thou didst bring into existence the universe, and through thy will it exists and was established."

COMMENTARY

The forces preside in turn over the time-periods; thus in the human aura a *tattva* rules each hour, its particular psychic color predominating in the aura during that time. Hence the Ancients are represented as worshipping before the throne, each making obeisance in turn and throwing down his crown, giving over his rule to the next.

CHAPTER V. 1, 2

I saw on the right hand of the [God] seated on the throne a scroll, written inside and on the back, securely sealed with seven seals. And I saw a strong Divinity proclaiming with a great voice:

"Who is worthy to open the scroll and force open its seals?"

COMMENTARY

The scroll is a mysterious document which it has taken the God æons to write, a Bible which, when rightly read, discloses cosmic and divine mysteries. It is simply the human body, and its seals are the force-centres wherein radiates the formative force of the Logos. These seals are the same as the seven Societies and the lampstands. The expression "written inside and on the back" refers to the cerebro-spinal axis and the great sympathetic system.

The "strong Divinity," as shown by the attributive adjective, is Kronos, the God of Time, who in mythology is the oldest of the twelve great Gods.

Ch. v. 3–5

No one—in the sky, on the earth, or under the earth—was able to open the scroll, or [even] to see it. I wept much because no worthy one was found to open the scroll, or [even] to see it! One of the Ancients says to me:

"Do not weep. Behold! the Lion, he of the tribe of Juda, the root of David, has conquered: [he is worthy] to open the scroll and its seven seals."

COMMENTARY

Here Iôannês indulges in one of the sarcastic hyperboles that are not infrequent in his *Evangel.* Those unable to open the *chakras* are usually ignorant of the fact that the body is the lyre of Apollo, the instrument of the Sun-Logos, and therefore do not see it in its real nature. Yet in his day spiritual blindness probably was less prevalent than in the present age, applied to which his statement becomes more nearly literal than hyperbolic.

The Lion is, of course, Leo, which is also the sign of Juda. The "root" of man is his spiritual Self; for the mystical "tree of life," man, is the inverted *ashvattha* tree, which has its roots in the heavens and its branches on the earth: therefore "the root of David" is David reincarnated.

Ch. v. 6, 7

I saw; and, Behold! in the midst of the throne and the four Beings, and in the midst of the Ancients, there was a Lamb standing, as if it had been sacrificed, having seven horns and seven eyes, which are the seven Breaths of the God, sent off into all the earth. He came—he has taken [the scroll] from the right hand of [the God] seated on the throne!

COMMENTARY

The Lamb is a variant of the Ram, Aries; and the "Lamb" here is identical with the "Lion of the tribe of Juda," since the sign Leo is the sole domicile of the Sun, and Aries is the place of his highest exaltation. Microcosmically, Leo corresponds to the *sahasrâra chakra,* the "third eye," and Aries to the nimbus, or cerebral radiance. This Lamb is the incarnated Nous, the intellectual Sun, which may be regarded as the Third Logos—man as he is on earth. The horns and eyes are the seven noetic powers of action and the seven noetic perceptive faculties. Thus the Lamb represents the neophyte, whose inner nature is awakening, and who is about to undergo the perfecting, or initiatory, ordeals.

CH. V. 8–10

When he had taken the scroll, the four Beings and the twenty-four Ancients fell down in front of the Lamb, having each a lyre and a golden libation-saucer full of incense-offerings, which are the prayers of the devotees. And they chanted a new lyric, saying:

"Worthy art thou to take the scroll and to open its seals; for thou wast sacrificed, and didst buy for the God with thy blood [the good qualities] from every tribe, tongue, nation and people, and didst make them [to be] a realm and sacrificers to our God; and they are ruling on the earth."

COMMENTARY

Each of the Ancients, as here described, has a saucer, the *phialê*, a discous cup used in pouring out drink-offerings to the Gods, and also, like Apollo, has a lyre. The *phialê* symbolizes the *chakra* ("disc"), or ganglion, and the lyre the nerve-fibres connected with it. Each *chakra* has its distinctive quality, color, sound and incense-odor, all of which are perceivable by the psychic senses. The four symbols employed in the four conquests, the seal, the trumpet, the sickle and the libation-saucer, appropriately represent the *chakras*.

The neophyte is worthy to take control of the marvellous psychic mechanism of the body, to "conquer" its *chakras*, tightening its slack organism till it is tense and vibrant as a lyre in the hands of a musician, because he has in many incarnations, in every nation and in many conditions of life, acquired the nobler characteristics of each and moulded them into a character—a kingdom, truly,—in which they are the ruling elements.

The chorus of praise by the four Beings and the twenty-four Ancients is the first of the seven choruses in the drama.

CH. V. 11–14

I saw; and I heard a voice of many Divinities around the throne, the Beings and the Ancients—there were myriads of myriads,—saying with a great voice:

"Worthy is the sacrificed Lamb to receive the force, wealth, skill, strength, honor, glory and praise."

Every existent being which is in the sky, on the earth, under the earth, and on the sea—the universe summed up in them—I heard saying:

"To the [God] seated on the throne, and to the Lamb, be the praise, the honor, the glory and the dominion throughout the æons of the æons!"

And the four Beings said "AMÊN." And the twenty-four Ancients fell down and worshipped [the God].

COMMENTARY

The three pæans chanted in praise of the Conqueror and his God are in accordance with the Greek custom of chanting pæans to Apollo, the Sun-God, before and after battle or before any solemn undertaking; and they are very appropriate here, since the Conqueror, the Lion-Lamb, stands for the Nous, or microcosmic Sun, and having taken the scroll he is about to undergo the ordeals of initiation; and the word Iêsous, which is but a mystery-name for the Nous, has a most suspicious resemblance to Iêios, the epithet applied to Apollo because he was invoked in the pæans by the reiterated cry "Iê," hailing him as the "Savior." Iêsous is evidently Iêios raised to 888, the Gnostic Ogdoad (the manifested Logos) in triune form.

The *Apocalypse* follows the style of the Greek tragedies in employing choruses to divide the drama into acts. Of these three choral songs, the first is chanted by the Beings and the Ancients, and in the second the lesser Divinities join in; both these pæans being in praise of the sacrificial Lamb; while the third song is a general chorus by all the powers and potencies of the microcosmic universe in praise of the Lamb and the enthroned God. The first pæan is merely explanatory, telling why the neophyte is worthy to open the seals; the second is an evocation of the potencies of the seven planets; and the third is addressed to the four higher planets only. All this means simply that the practical student of the sacred science, the neophyte, is here engaged in the mystic meditation: with exalted mind and feeling he evokes the *paraklêtos* in its active form as the *speirêma*, the serpent-force that opens the seven planetary centres, or "seven seals."

CHAPTER VI. 1, 2

I saw, when the Lamb opened one of the seven seals, and I heard one of the four Beings saying as with a voice of thunder:

"Come!"

I saw; and, Behold! a white horse [came out]. The [Divinity] who was riding him had a bow; to him was given a crown, and he came forth a conqueror, and that he might keep on conquering.

COMMENTARY

This seal is the *adhishthâna chakra,* the prostatic, where the positive and negative currents start. It corresponds to Sagittarius; hence its rider, or regent, is the Bowman. In this sign the Romans placed Diana, the Greek Lêtôïs, Apollo's sister, who was sometimes pictured as a bearded Goddess; together they represent the male-female or androgynous man. This *chakra* belongs to the lowest of the somatic divisions; yet, as the white horse, that division outranks the others, and the Bowman, Apollo-Diana, is the Conqueror himself, who is here represented as starting out on his conquests, and who reappears in triumph in the closing scene of the drama. For the Logos, as mirrored in the material world, is inverted.

Seal .

CH. VI. 3, 4

When he opened the second seal, I heard the second Being saying:

"Come!"

Another horse, fiery-red, came out. To the [Divinity] who was riding him [authority] was given to take away peace from the earth—that

[men] should slaughter one another—and to him was given a great sword.

COMMENTARY

This seal is the epigastric *chakra*, and its sign is Scorpio, the house of Mars, the War-God. Scorpio is usually, but inaccurately, given as corresponding to the generative centres; but the real seat of the epithumetic nature is the solar plexus. The red horse represents the abdominal somatic division, and its rider, or regent, who is passion personified, appears later in the drama in the rôle of the red Dragon, who is identified with Satan and Diabolos, the "Devil."

CH. VI. 5, 6

When he opened the third seal, I heard the third Being saying:

"Come!"

I saw; and, Behold! a black horse [came out]. The [Divinity] who was riding him had a balance in his hand. I heard as it were a voice in the midst of the four Beings saying:

"A ration of wheat for a *denarius*, and three rations of barley for a *denarius*—and do scant justice to the olive-oil and the wine!"

COMMENTARY

Here it is the cardiac *chakra* that is opened; it corresponds to Libra, and the regent of this somatic division is the Weigher, the discursive lower mind. Although no actual thinking process takes place in the heart, a distinction is drawn between the spiritual mind, or pure intellection, and the unspiritual mind, or that portion of the intellectual nature which is tainted by psychic emotions and carnal desires, or, in other words, between the mind that reflects the light which comes from above, from the Nous, and the mind that absorbs the influences that come from below, from the animal nature. This lower intellectual sphere may include the greatest culture, with admirable attainments in scientific research and in the acquisition of knowledge, along conventional lines, yet with little or no spiritual insight or philosophic depth of thought; hence it is depicted in the allegory as a semi-famine, a scarcity of rations. The parsimonious Weigher who rides the black horse appears later in the drama as the Beast, the marine monster in whom fanciful theology sees the Anti-Christ.

CH. VI. 7, 8

When he opened the fourth seal, I heard the voice of the fourth Being saying:

"Come!"

I saw; and, Behold! a dun horse [came out]. The [Divinity] who was riding him—his name was Death, and the Unseen went along with him. To them was given authority over the fourth of the earth, to kill with sword, famine and death, and by the wild beasts of the earth.

COMMENTARY

The laryngeal *chakra* is the highest of the ones belonging strictly to the sympathetic system, the ones above it being in the brain. It is here given as the regent of the highest of the somatic divisions, the "sky," or rather the *lower* sky, for the cerebral region is termed in the *Apocalypse* the mid-sky, or zenith, as being the abode of the God. Plato, in the *Phaidros,* employs in his allegory two horses, answering to the intellectual and the epithumetic natures, the Nous being the charioteer; but usually the chariot of the Sun was pictured with four horses.

The vocal apparatus is, mystically, the creative organ of the Logos; and for this and other reasons the white and the dun horses are given with their attributes interchanged. The dun horse represents the lowest of the somatic divisions; and as sex exists only in the physical and psychic worlds, the two, Death and Hadês (standing for the generative principle on the two planes) are his riders, who slay with sword, famine, materialism and animal passions. They reappear later in the form of the two-horned bogus Lamb, who is called the Pseudo-Seer.

CH. VI. 9–11

When he opened the fifth seal, I saw underneath the altar the souls of those who had been sacrificed because of the arcane doctrine of the God, and because of the evidence which they had. They cried out with a great voice, saying:

"How long, O thou the Supreme, the Holy and the True, dost thou fail to judge and avenge our blood upon those who dwell on the earth?"

White robes were given them severally, and it was said to them that they should keep still yet a little time, until their fellow-slaves and also their brothers, who would be killed even as they were, should have finished [their course].

COMMENTARY

The fifth seal corresponds to the sign Cancer and the *âjñâ chakra*, or cavernous plexus, which latter is closely connected with the pituitary body, the *membrum virile*, so to say, of the brain. The atrophied ("sacrificed") brain-centres are partially aroused by the *speirêma* at this stage; but they are suppressed until the other centres (their "brothers") have all been brought into action and then "killed," that is, placed in abeyance while the cerebral centres are being awakened. They receive "white robes," however, for at this centre the currents bifurcate and their light suffuses the brain.

During the cycle of reincarnation, all the *chakras* have been slain by the gross elements of the material, sensuous life; yet they retain the "evidence" of things spiritual.

Although Leo precedes Cancer, the order in which the *chakras* are awakened is different; for Capricorn and Leo belong rather to the spinal axis than to the sympathetic system, and are the two poles of the former.

CH. VI. 12–17

I saw when he opened the sixth seal; and, Behold! there came to be a great earthquake; the sun became dark as a sack [woven of camel's] hair; the moon became as blood, and the stars of the sky fell to the earth, as a fig-tree drops her first-crop figs when shaken by a violent wind. The sky was removed like a scroll being rolled up; and every mountain and island—they were moved from their places! The rulers of the earth, the very great, the commanders, the rich, and the mighty, and every slave and freeman, hid themselves in the caves and among the crags of the mountains; and they kept saying to the mountains and the crags:

"Fall on us and hide us from the face of the [God] seated on the throne and from the passion of the Lamb! For the great day of his passion has come, and who can stand firm?"

COMMENTARY

This sixth seal is the *mûlâdhâra chakra*, which lies at the base of the spinal cord and is the starting-point of the central current, the *sushumnâ*, the regenerative force, here called the *ôrgê* (fecundating energy) of the "Lamb," the Nous. Upon the outpouring of this fiery electric force into the brain, the mind becomes blank and the novice is conscious only of blind terror; this is allegorized as the darkening of the sun (the mind), the falling of the stars (the thoughts), the vanishing of the sky (the concept of space), and the panic of the earth-dwellers (the lower forces and faculties).

CHAPTER VII. 1–3

After these [ordeals] I saw four Divinities standing at the four corners of the earth, dominating the four winds of the earth so that no wind should blow on the earth or the sea, or on any tree. And I saw another [dominant] Divinity ascend from the birth-place of the sun, having the signet-ring of the living God; and he cried out with a great voice to the four Divinities to whom [authority] was given to punish the earth and the sea, saying:

"Do not punish the earth, the sea or the trees till we shall have sealed [with his signet-ring] the slaves of our God on their foreheads."

COMMENTARY

These five Divinities are the noetic regents of the five *prânas,* the solar life-winds. They are represented in the zodiac by the signs Gemini, Taurus, Aries, Pisces and Aquarius, with their respective planets. The four who guard the quarters are the four powers of the Nous; and the fifth, who rises up from the sun's place of birth (*anatolê*), is the representative of the Nous himself, and therefore bears the signet of the Life-God. They correspond to the "five bright powers" of the *Upanishads*, four of which are regents of the four directions of space, while the fifth "goes upward to immortality." It is these noetic forces that record in the aura of man (his "scroll of life") his every thought and deed; and, as these auric impressions, like phonographic records, automatically reproduce the original thoughts and emotions whenever the forces again act upon them, they thus produce an almost endless concatenation of cause and effect, of retributive action. Therefore, by awakening the occult forces of his nature the neophyte invokes this iron law of retribution, and all the good and evil elements of his nature are arrayed against each other for the final conflict. In the allegory the lower principles are to be chastised, and the higher ones are to be given the seal of the God's approval.

CH. VII. 4–8

I heard the number of those who were sealed, one hundred and forty-four thousand, sealed out of all the tribes of the children of Israel: of the tribe of Juda were sealed twelve thousand; of the tribe of Reuben, twelve thousand; of the tribe of Gad, twelve thousand; of the tribe of Asher, twelve thousand; of the tribe of Naphtali, twelve thousand; of the tribe of Manasseh, twelve thousand; of the tribe of Simeon, twelve thousand; of the tribe of Levi, twelve thousand; of the tribe of Issachar, twelve thousand; of the tribe of Zebulon, twelve thousand; of the tribe of Joseph, twelve thousand; and of the tribe of Benjamin, twelve thousand.

COMMENTARY

The tribes stand for the twelve signs of the zodiac, Juda for Leo, Reuben for Aquarius, Gad for Aries, etc.; but as here given by Iôannês, Joseph is substituted for Ephraim, or Taurus; and Manasseh, Joseph's firstborn son, replaces Dan, who is Scorpio. This omission of Dan, with the substitutions by which Scorpio is shown to be derived from Taurus, is significant; for Taurus is the symbol of celestial creative force, and Scorpio that of the generative function. The Divinities charged with the seven scourges are, astronomically, the seven Pleiades, a star-group in the constellation Taurus. There was a Jewish tradition that from the tribe of Dan was to come the Anti-Messias; hence the substitution of the paranatellon Aquila for Scorpio.

CH. VII. 9–12

After these [things] I saw; and, Behold! a vast multitude, which no one could count, from among every people, and of [all] tribes, nations and tongues, [were] standing before the throne and before the Lamb, wearing white robes and [carrying] palm-branches in their hands. They kept crying out with a great voice, saying:

"The deliverance is to the [Master] seated on the throne of our God, and to the Lamb!"

All the Divinities were standing in a circle about the throne, the Ancients and the four Beings; they fell on their faces in front of the throne, and worshipped the God, saying:

"AMÊN. The praise, the glory, the skill, the thanks, the honor, the force and the strength be to our God throughout the æons of the æons! AMÊN."

COMMENTARY

This is the third of the seven choruses; the verse, or pæan of praise, is chanted by the liberated elements, and the chorus by the ruling powers of the three worlds—the Beings, Ancients and Divinities forming three concentric circles about the throne, and thus representing as many planes of manifestation. In the benediction the attributes of all the seven planets are ascribed to the Sun-God.

CH. VII. 13–17

One of the Ancients responded, saying to me:

"These who are wearing the white robes—who are they, and whence did they come?"

I said to him:

"My Master, *you* know."

He said to me:

"These are the [Conquerors] coming out of the great ordeal. They washed their robes and bleached them in the Lamb's blood. Because of this, they are before the throne of the God; and they are serving him day and night in his adytum, and the [Master] seated on the throne will spread his tent over them. They will hunger no more, thirst no more; neither will [the rays of] the sun beat down on them, nor any scorching heat. For the Lamb who is in the middle of the throne will shepherd them and guide them to springs of waters of life, and the God will wipe away every tear from their eyes."

COMMENTARY

The great ordeal of the soul, or Logos, is its incarceration in the carnal body, not merely for the term of one short lifetime, but during a long series of incarnations throughout the æons of generation; but the Logos has its own mighty purpose in thus crucifying itself by assuming the human form, descending into the spheres of generation and passing through the vast "cycle of necessity": it builds up for itself, out of the elements of the lower worlds, an outer self, a being formed of the "dust of the earth," the refuse of past cycles, yet having within it the breath of the God; and then by unremitting toil throughout the æons it refines and transmutes the elements of this creature (who is the carnal, animal-human man) until it redeems it, and it becomes one with the divine individuality. These purified and redeemed principles of the lower self are the countless host who, now that the aspirant has entered upon the cycle of initiation, the final "perfecting" or "finishing" labor, are coming out of "the great ordeal," singing pæans of praise to the sacrificial Lamb, the Crucified, and to the enthroned Self, the Eternal, who is beyond change and time, and therefore "uncrucified."

CHAPTER VIII. 1–6

When he opened the seventh seal, there came to be silence in the sky for about half an hour.

I saw the seven Divinities who stand before the God. To them were given seven trumpets. Came another Divinity and stationed himself above the altar, having a golden censer; and to him was given much incense, that he might offer it, with the prayers of all the devotees, upon the golden altar in front of the throne. The smoke of the incense, with the prayers of the devotees, went up in front of the God out of the Divinity's hand. The Divinity took the censer and filled it with the fire of the altar, and cast [the fire] into the earth: there came to be voices, thunders, lightnings and an earthquake. The seven Divinities having the seven trumpets made themselves ready to give the trumpet-calls.

COMMENTARY

The seventh seal is the *sahasrâra chakra,* to which corresponds the sign Leo, the sole domicile of the Sun. This *chakra,* the conarium, or pineal body, is the "third eye" of the seer—that, and much more. It is the focal point of all the forces of the nervous system and of the aura; here they come to an equilibrium, and here reigns the mystic Silence. During the meditation, as each *chakra* is awakened the neophyte sees its corresponding psychic color; and at this seventh centre the colors intermingle as in an opal, with an incessant glittering of white light playing as on the facets of a diamond. The psychic senses of smell and hearing begin to be aroused, so that odors as of incense become perceptible, and mysterious sounds are heard; then with a shock that Iôannês here compares to an earthquake the forces start upon the circuit of the seven brain-centres, each of which when the current reaches it produces a vibrant sound in the aura, the "trumpet-call" of the allegory.

The sounding of the trumpets follows the exact order of the opening of the seals; and the two series correspond throughout, the zodiacal signs being repeated as related to the brain-centres.

CH. VIII. 7

The first [Divinity] gave the trumpet-call. There came to be hail and fire, mixed with blood; they were cast into the earth, and the third of the earth was burnt up, the third of the trees was burnt up, and all fresh grass was burnt up.

COMMENTARY

Of the four planes of consciousness, the fourth, the physical, was stilled, or temporarily suppressed, by the opening of the "seals," and the psychic became active; now, by the awakening of the noetic centres the psychic consciousness—"the third"—is in turn placed in abeyance. The colors manifested by the centres of the sympathetic system are psychic; the sounds heard upon the opening of the brain-centres pertain to a higher plane.

Trumpet

The "hail" is a semi-condensation of the lunar element, or ether, "the good water of the Moon"; the "fire" is the solar force, "the good fire of the Sun"; and the "blood" is the auric fluid, "the blood of the Logos." These three elements affect the lowest of the divisions; the "trees" are the "two olive-trees" (the dual tree of life), and the "grass" is the radiation of the same force through the aureola. They are, of course, the threefold *speirêma*, starting on its course through the brain.

CH. VIII. 8, 9

The second Divinity gave the trumpet-call. [It was] as if a great flaming mountain of fire was cast into the sea; and the third of the sea came to be blood. The third of the existent beings in the sea —having souls—died; and the third of the ships were wrecked.

COMMENTARY

The active volcano is a symbol of Mars, the planetary force ruling the epithumetic nature, "the sea."

CH. VIII. 10, 11

The third Divinity gave the trumpet-call. There fell from the sky a great star flaming like a torch. It fell on the third of the rivers and on the springs of waters. The name of the star is called "Wormwood"; and the third of the waters became wormwood, and many of the men died of the waters, because they were made bitter.

COMMENTARY

The falling star is Aphroditê (Venus), ἡ Φωσφόρος (Lucifer), the torch-bearing Goddess. The force it here symbolizes affects the emotional psychic nature; and the imbittering of the waters alludes to the psychological law that all pleasure eventually reacts and becomes pain; yet, in the end, this bitter water becomes transmuted into the "sweet water of life" when man's nature is purified.

CH. VIII. 12

The fourth Divinity gave the trumpet-call. The third of the sun was stricken, also the third of the moon and the third of the stars, so that the third of them should be darkened, and the day should not give light for the third of it, and likewise the night.

COMMENTARY

All mental action is here suspended on the psychic, or subjective, plane, as well as on the material, or objective. On each plane, in turn, the forces have to be brought into equilibrium, so that they neutralize each other, and then the consciousness rises to the next higher plane.

CH. VIII. 13

I saw; and I heard a lone Eagle, flying in mid-sky, saying with a great voice:

"Woe, woe, woe to those dwelling on the earth, from the remaining trumpet-voices of the three Divinities who are about to give the trumpet-call!"

COMMENTARY

The first four cerebral *chakras* (symbolized by the trumpets) react upon the four somatic divisions; the three higher ones are related to the dual nervous system and the aura, broadly speaking; but in a more special sense they are analogues of the male creative triad. Comment on this subject, which is a delicate one, though involving nothing that is in the slightest degree impure, must be necessarily brief and somewhat superficial in a work that is designed for general circulation. As has already been pointed out, the lower man is an inverted image of the higher; and from this it follows that the highest spiritual centres are directly related to the lowest, the creative centres on the material plane. For this reason the three trumpet-calls are announced as "woes" by the Eagle, the fourth of the *Zôa*, who is the prototype of Scorpio. It can not be too emphatically reiterated that the sex-function exists only in the physical and psychic worlds; and the impure forces related to it are not employed in any way or for any purpose whatever by the followers of the Gnôsis. The abuse of this function is the most terrible of all crimes, the "blasphemy against the holy Pneuma," and the "unpardonable sin"—the punishment of which by natural law is the annihilation of the individuality, the "second death." It is only the celibates, who preserve the utmost purity of mind and body, thereby regaining the complete innocence of "little children," who can hope to "enter the kingdom of heaven."

CHAPTER IX. 1–12

The fifth Divinity gave the trumpet-call. I saw a star that has fallen from the sky to the earth; and to him was given the key to the crater of the abyss. He opened the crater of the abyss, and there went up smoke from the crater, like the smoke of a great furnace. The sun and the air were darkened by the smoke from the crater. Out of the smoke came locusts upon the earth, and to them was given license as the scorpions of the earth have license. It was said to them that they should not punish the grass of the earth, neither anything tender-green nor any tree, but only those men who do not have the seal of the God on their foreheads; and [the command] was given them that they should not kill them, but that they should be tormented five months. Their torment was as a scorpion's torment when it stings a man. In those days men will seek death, and find it not; they will long to die, and death will keep fleeing from them! The effigies of the locusts were like horses caparisoned for battle. On their heads were [circlets] like crowns of spurious gold. Their faces were like men's faces, but they had hair like women's hair; and their teeth were like [the teeth] of lions. They had cuirasses like iron cuirasses. The voice of their wings was like the voice of [many] war-chariots—of many horses galloping into battle. They have tails like scorpions, and stings were in their tails. Their license to punish men was five months. They have over them as ruler the Divinity of the Abyss; his name in Hebrew is *Abaddôn,* and in the Greek [mysticism] he has the name *Apollyôn.*

The one woe has passed. Behold! two more woes are coming after.

COMMENTARY

The star that has fallen is Venus, now become the so-called "infernal Lucifer," the Hecatê who presides over the abyss. This abyss is represented astronomically by the constellation Crater, the Cup, the mixing-bowl of Iacchos, the phallic God. It appears also in the *Apocalypse* as the cup held by the Woman in scarlet, who simply is Hecatê, the infernal aspect of both Aphroditê (Venus) and

Lêtôïs (Diana), the two Goddesses alike symbolizing the primordial substance, the Archê.

The Divinity of the Abyss, who is the "Destroyer" and the "Murderer," is the Pseudo-Lion, the Beast—the phrênic mind polluted by the carnal passions; and his hordes of scorpion-like cavalry are impure and unholy thoughts. The "five months" are the summertime, during which period the passional nature is more active: mystically the summer is said to be the night of the soul, and winter its day.

CH. IX. 13–15

The sixth Divinity gave the trumpet-call. I heard a single voice from the four horns of the golden altar in front of the God, [the Master's voice], saying to the sixth Divinity, who had the trumpet:

"Turn loose the four Divinities who are fettered at the great river Euphrates."

The four Divinities were turned loose, who had been made ready throughout the hour, day, month and year, that they should kill the third of men.

COMMENTARY

The golden altar is the Nous, or higher mind, and the four horns are its four powers. Gold is the metal of the sun, and the four-horned altar is but a different symbol for the sun and the regents of the four quarters. The four Divinities fettered at the river Euphrates (the cerebro-spinal axis) are the *prânas*.

Ch. ix. 16–21

The number of the armies of the horsemen [under the command of the four Divinities] was two hundred million—I heard the number of them. Thus I saw the horses in the vision, and their riders, having cuirasses fiery [red], smoky blue and sulphurous [yellow]: the heads of the horses were like the heads of lions, and from their mouths keep going out fire, smoke and sulphur. By these three scourges were killed the third of the men—by the fire, the smoke and the sulphur which went out of their mouths. For the powers of the horses are in their mouths and in their tails; for their tails are like snakes, and have heads, and with them they inflict punishment. The rest of the men, who were not killed by these scourges, did not reform from the works of their hands, that they should not worship the spirits and the images of gold, silver, bronze, stone and wood, which can neither see, hear nor walk. And they did not reform from their murders, their sorceries, their prostitutions or their thefts.

COMMENTARY

The vast armies of horsemen in armor represent the limitless powers of the Nous; the lion-heads of the horses indicating their solar character. As the Mind is the real man, so in the allegory the intellectual powers and thoughts are represented as men, the armies of the Nous destroying the evil, false, superstitious thoughts and tendencies of the psychic nature; and as the thoughts of the carnal mind are concerned largely with material possessions, such thoughts are referred to as worshippers of idols.

CHAPTER X. 1–4

I saw another, [the] strong Divinity, coming down out of the sky, wrapped in a cloud, and a rainbow was upon his head. His face was [luminous] like the sun, and his feet like pillars of fire. In his hand he had a little scroll unrolled. He placed his right foot on the sea, and the left on the earth, and cried out with a great voice, as a lion roars; and when he cried out, seven thunders uttered voices of their own. And when the seven thunders uttered [their voices], I was about to write down [the teachings]; but I heard a voice from the sky saying to me:

"Seal up [the teachings] which the seven thunders uttered, and do not write them down."

COMMENTARY

The Divinity, the fifth in the group, is the Nous, the intellectual Sun, in its aspect as Kronos, the God of Time. This fivefold group is the same as that which appeared upon the opening of the sixth seal, save that here they are energizing on a higher plane.

That the voices of the seven thunders were mystery-teachings is evident from the injunction by the Initiator against recording them.

CH. X. 5–7

The Divinity whom I saw standing on the sea and on the earth raised his right hand to the sky and swore by the [God] who lives throughout the æons of the æons, who brought into existence the sky and what is in it, the earth and what is in it, and the sea and what is in it, that Time shall be no more, but in the days of the voice of the seventh Divinity, when he is about to give the trumpet-call, also shall be made perfect the Mystery of the God, as he proclaimed to his slaves, the seers.

COMMENTARY

Time, the "image of eternity," rules in the physical and psychic worlds, the earth and the sea of the allegory; but in the spiritual world, the mystic "sky," there is the timeless, eternal consciousness of the God. The seventh trumpet-call signalizes the opening of that "Mystery of the God," the "eye" of the seer, which is made perfect, that is, restored to its spiritual functions, by the action of the *speirêma*.

CH. X. 8–11

The voice that I heard from the sky—[I heard it] again speaking with me, and saying:

"Go; take the little scroll unrolled in the hand of the Divinity who is standing on the sea and on the earth."

I went to the Divinity, asking him to give me the little scroll. He says to me:

"Take it, and eat it up. It will make your belly bitter; but in your mouth it will be sweet as honey."

I took the little scroll from the hand of the Divinity, and ate it up. In my mouth it was as honey, sweet; but when I had eaten it my belly was made bitter. And [the voices of the seven thunders] keep saying to me:

"You must teach again in opposition to many nations, peoples, tongues and rulers."

COMMENTARY

The little scroll is the Gnôsis, imparted to the neophyte by the Initiator—his own Logos. When the instruction is assimilated, that is, carried out in practice, it becomes bitter to the epithumetic nature, since it inculcates the extirpation of every impure thought and desire.

Kronos represents the Logos in his aspect as Memory, and therefore holds the scroll of the Gnôsis, since all true knowledge is spiritual reminiscence.

Although forbidden to record the utterances of the seven thunders (the theurgic teachings), the seer is under an obligation to proclaim the true philosophy and ethics in opposition to the popular dogmas of the exoteric religions.

CHAPTER XI. 1–3

There was given me a reed like a wand, [the first voice] saying:

"Rise up, and measure the adytum of the God, the altar, and those worshipping in it; but the court which is exterior to the adytum cast out as exoteric, and do not measure it; for it has been given to the people, and the holy city they shall trample on for forty-two months. I shall give it [after that] to my two witnesses, and they will teach one thousand two hundred and sixty days, clothed in gunny-sacks."

COMMENTARY

The *naos*, here translated adytum, was the inner temple, or sanctuary, where the God was enshrined, and to which none but the initiated had access; when employed for initiatory rites it was usually called the *adyton*. Symbolically, the adytum is the spiritual nature, and the altar the intellectual; astronomically, it is, as Josephus and other ancient writers said, the sky. But in the psycho-physiological rendering of the symbolism the adytum, the altar of sacrifice and the altar of incense are the three divisions of the brain, and the outer court is the body. The worshippers are the forty-nine forces, which are "measured" by being arranged in hierarchies, or groups, as shown on page 70.

The period of initiation is here placed at seven years, during the first half of which (forty-two months, or three and one-half years) the lower forces continue to rule the functions of the body, while in the latter half (one thousand two hundred and sixty days, again three and one-half years) the dual electric force, *îdâ* and *pingala,* the "two witnesses," will pervade the nervous system, gradually and almost imperceptibly replacing the ordinary nerve-force, a subdued action which is expressed in the allegory by their being wrapped in gunny-sacks.

The measuring of the adytum and the account of the two witnesses have nothing to do with the action of the drama, but are merely explanatory.

CH. XI. 4–6

These are the two olive-trees, and two little lampstands, standing before the God of the earth. If any one wills to use them wrongfully, fire comes out of their mouth and devours their enemies; and if any one shall will to use them wrongfully, in this way must he be killed. These [witnesses] have authority to shut the sky, so that rain may not shower down during the days of their teaching; also they have authority over the waters, to transmute them into blood, and to chastise the earth with every scourge, as often as they may will.

COMMENTARY

Zechariah (iv. 2 *et seq.*) goes more into detail concerning the two olive-trees and the lampstands that stand before the Earth-God: "I have seen; and, Behold! a candlestick all of gold, with its bowl upon the top of it, and its seven lamps thereon; there are seven pipes to each of the lamps, which are upon the top thereof: and two olive-trees by it, one upon the right side of the bowl, and the other upon the left side thereof." These are the cerebral *chakras* and their *nâdîs;* and, as they are very small and seemingly unimportant, he continues: "For who hath despised the day of small things? For they [the seven] shall rejoice, and shall see the plummet in the hand of Zerubbabel, even these seven [which are] the eyes of Jehovah; they run to and fro through the whole earth." The plummet of Zerubbabel, who was the builder of the temple, is the pituitary organ, which controls the growth of the entire body. As modern physiologists have demonstrated, the disease called gigantism, in which the body or any of its members grow to abnormal size, is due to the over-activity and enlargement of the pituitary. It is the creative organ of the brain; and when energized by the *speirêma* its pulsating aura takes on a swinging motion, like a plummet, until it impinges on the conarium, "the unpaired eye," impregnating it with the golden force and arousing the spiritual faculties. This action is further described by Zechariah, who says that "the two olive-trees" and "the two olive branches which are beside the two golden spouts, that empty the golden [oil] out of themselves" are "the two anointed ones, that stand by the Lord of the whole earth."

The dual fire is destructive to the unpurified psychic or sorcerer who may succeed in arousing it, and its wrongful use results in moral as well as physical death.

By "rain" the nerve-fluid is symbolized; "water" is the magnetic, auric substance, and "blood" the golden electric fire. The "chastisement" of the earth is described, later on in the drama, as the pouring out of seven scourges by the seven Taurine Divinities, the Pleiades.

CH. XI. 7

When they shall have finished giving their evidence, the Beast who comes up out of the abyss will battle with them, conquer them, and kill them.

COMMENTARY

When the trance is ended, and the neophyte returns to the ordinary state of consciousness on the material plane, the *kundalinî* recedes to the "throne of the Beast," the solar plexus, where it is said in the *Upanishads* to lie coiled up like a slumbering serpent, having three and a half coils, corresponding to the three and a half measures of the *Aum*.

CH. XI. 8, 9

Their corpses [are now lying] in the main-street of the great city which mystically is called "Sodom" and "Egypt," where also their Master was crucified. And [some] from among the nations, tribes, tongues and peoples are guarding their corpses three and a half days, and will not permit their dead bodies to be placed in a sepulchre.

COMMENTARY

The city is the physical body, and its main-street is the spinal cord, in which are the channels of the threefold *speirêma,* the two witnesses and their Master, "the Witness Believable and True"; and these channels—the "corpses" of the witnesses—are preserved from complete atrophy by those nerve-currents which, in each of the four somatic divisions, circulate through the cerebro-spinal system. The three and a half days are the latter half of the seven "days of creation," the gross material arc of the cycle of human evolution, during which the "witnesses" are lying moribund in the mystical "Sodom."

The formula "nations, tribes, tongues and peoples" is given seven times in the *Apocalypse,* but the words are never twice in the same order; in one instance (x. 11) "rulers" is substituted for "tribes," and in another (xvii. 15) "multitudes" for the same. They apply to the four castes, or classes of mankind, who in oriental mysticism are said to have been born from the four somatic divisions of the Deity: men of learning, warriors, commercialists and laborers.

Iêsous, the Nous, is here said to have been crucified in Sodom, also called Egypt: this is the first crucifixion, the incarnation of the soul in the physical body, which is then its cross. The second is in Calvaria (*kranion*), on the cross of initiation.

CH. XI. 10–14

Those who dwell on the earth are rejoicing over them and are exultant; and they will send bribes to one another—for those two seers did torment those who are dwelling on the earth! After the three and a half days the Breath of Life from the God entered into them; they stood on their feet, and great terror overcame those who beheld them. They heard a great voice from the sky saying to them:

"Come up hither."

They went up into the sky in the cloud; and their enemies beheld them. In that hour there came to be a great earthquake, and the tenth [section] of the city fell, and there were killed by the earthquake names of men seven thousand; the rest became frightened, and gave glory to the God of the sky.

The second woe has passed. Behold! the third woe is coming speedily.

COMMENTARY

The rebuking voice of conscience, which is the voice of the Nous speaking through the "two witnesses," is the real tormentor of the evilly disposed, who seek ever to stifle it; and the man who is thus trying to silence his accusing conscience can not be mentally honest with himself, but acts from feigned motives, his desires and thoughts bribing one another, as the allegory puts it. But as the individual emerges from the materialistic stage of his evolution, the noetic faculties "awaken from the dead," and the base passional nature, symbolized by the tenth of the twelve zodiacal divisions, perishes, with its seven heads, for it is identified with the seven-headed red Dragon. The seven is multiplied by the indefinite number one thousand to indicate the many correlations of these lower principles, the "men," whose "names" are their psychic colors, which are obliterated, the remaining colors becoming brighter in the auric "glory" of the Sky-God.

CH. XI. 15–18

The seventh Divinity gave the trumpet-call. There came to be great voices in the sky, saying:

"The realm of the world has become [the realm] of our Master and of his Anointed, and he shall reign throughout the æons of the æons."

The twenty-four Ancients who are seated before the God on their thrones fell on their faces and worshipped the God, saying:

"We give thanks to thee, the Master-God, the All-Dominator, who [for ever] art, and who wast, because thou hast taken thy great force and regained sovereignty. The people grew passionate; and *thy* passion came, and the season of the dead to be judged, and [the season] to give their recompense to thy slaves the seers, to the devotees, and to those who fear thy name, the small and the great, and to destroy those who are destroying the earth."

COMMENTARY

The seventh of the mystic "spiritual sounds" signalizes the awakening of the highest of the *chakras*, the centres through which radiates the Light of the Logos. The passion of the God is not his "wrath," but is the creative energy of the Logos, the "great force" (*dynamis*) which produces the "birth from above"; and it is here placed in contrast with the passions that "are destroying the earth."

The chorus by the sky-voices and the Ancients is the fourth of the series.

Ch. xi. 19

The adytum of the God in the sky was opened, and in his adytum was seen the ark [containing the emblems] of his compact; and there came to be lightnings, voices, thunders, an earthquake and great hail.

COMMENTARY

The word *kibôtos*, properly meaning a wooden box, or coffer, is applied in the *New Testament* to the ark in the temple, as here, and also to the Noachian ark. The constellation Arca, the celestial Ship, situated to the south of Virgo, was also called *kibôtos* and "Noah's Ark." As exoteric exponents of phallicism are fond of pointing out, the ark is a symbol of the womb, the place of birth—which is perfectly true if it is regarded as merely a concrete symbol. But esoterically it has no such phallic significance, but stands for the exact opposite, the place of *spiritual rebirth*, the emergence into immortality. All mysticism aside, it symbolizes the womb in the brain, the latter being an androgynous organ wherein is immaculately conceived the *permanent* spiritual vehicle, the solar body.

CHAPTER XII. 1, 2

A great constellation was seen in the sky: a [winged] Woman clothed with the sun, the moon underneath her feet, and on her head a crown of twelve stars. She had [a babe] in her womb—and she keeps crying out, in the pangs of child-birth, racked with pain of parturition.

COMMENTARY

The seventh trumpet-call is the sound heard when the conarium is energized, and the latter corresponds to the sign Leo, the house of the Sun; but the constellation here disclosed is triadic, including in the symbol the signs Virgo (the house of Mercury), Leo and Cancer (the domicile of the Moon). Thus associated, Virgo figures as the Virgin Mother, who immaculately conceives and gives birth to the Son of the God; whereas, taken in combination with Libra (the house of Venus), and Scorpio (the house of Mars), she becomes the scarlet prostitute, the symbol of carnal generation. As

Virgo

the World-Mother, the White Virgin of the Skies, whether called Diana, Aphroditê, or Mary, she is the pure ether, the Logos-Light, or primordial force-substance; and as the Fallen Woman, the Queen of the Abyss, she is the parturient energy of nature, the basis of physical life, and as such she is named in the *Apocalypse* Sodom, Babylon and Egypt, merely to make her threefold like her celestial prototype, for in reality she includes all cities and countries inhabited by sinful mankind.

The word *sêmeion* (the synonym of *sêma*), in the Greek text, is the correct technical word for "constellation."

Virgo was always pictured with wings; and later in the text she has the two wings of the Eagle.

Ch. xii. 3–6

Another constellation was seen in the sky—and, Behold! a great fiery-red Dragon, having seven heads and ten horns, and on his heads seven diadems. His tail was trailing along the third of the stars of the sky and kept throwing them to the earth. The Dragon was standing in front of the Woman who was on the verge of parturition, so that as soon as she gave birth he might devour her child. She gave birth to a son, virile, who is destined to shepherd all the people with an iron wand; and her child was snatched up to the God and to his throne. The Woman fled into the desert, where she has a place made ready by the God, that there [the Divinities] may nourish her one thousand two hundred and sixty days.

COMMENTARY

This constellatory symbol is Draco, the pole Dragon, which has seven distinguishing stars, and which, as depicted in the ancient star-maps, extends over seven of the zodiacal signs, and in setting apparently sweeps a third of the starry sky down to the horizon. Microcosmically it symbolizes the passional nature, *epithumia*, the Apocalyptic number of which is 555. The energizing of the cerebral centres produces a reflex action in the lower nature, and unless the neophyte is duly purified the Dragon will indeed devour the child, not at the time of its birth, but at the moment when it is conceived. For the solar body is not born at this point, but only has its inception; though the psychic form may be projected. In the pagan Greek mysteries this stage of the telestic work was represented quite baldly as the generative act, but Iôannês has handled the subject more delicately, by substituting for the solar the psychic body, which is "born" with the physical body and grows conjointly with it. In the Apoca-

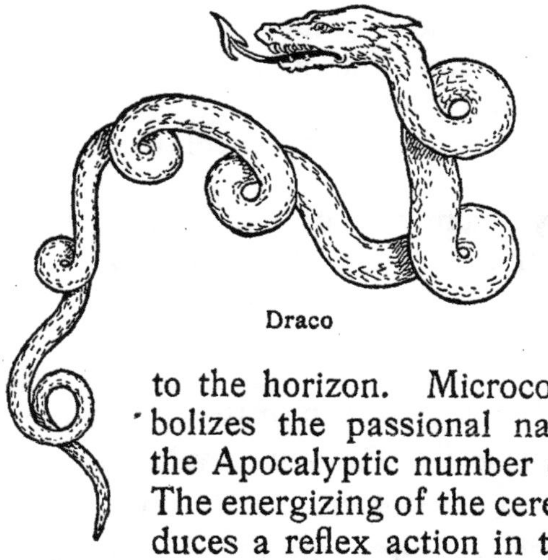

Draco

lyptic allegory the Conqueror is not born until after the three and a half years (the 1260 days) during which the Woman is being nourished by the Divinities; and the statement that the child is caught up to the *throne* connotes a period of spiritual gestation. In fact, the immaculate conception is here represented by the opening of the adytum and disclosure of the ark; and those who have investigated the subject of the ark need not be reminded of what were the very peculiar emblems it contained.

CH. XII. 7–12

There came to be a battle in the sky. Mikael and his Divinities gave battle to the Dragon; and the Dragon and his Divinities gave battle, but they lacked strength, nor was their place found in the sky any more. Hurled down was the great Dragon, the archaic Snake, who is called the "Accuser" and the "Adversary," the deluder of the whole inhabited earth; he was hurled down to the earth, and his Divinities were hurled down with him. I heard a great voice in the sky, saying:

"Now are attained the deliverance, the force and the ruling of our God, and the authority of his Anointed. For hurled down is the prosecutor of our brothers, who keeps prosecuting them before our God day and night. But they conquered him through the blood of the Lamb, and through the arcane doctrine of his evidence; and they did not esteem their psychic bodies until death. Therefore rejoice, ye skies, and ye who are pitching tent in them; [but] woe to the earth and the sea—for the Accuser has gone down to you having great lust, knowing that he has but a short season."

COMMENTARY

The Greek of the *Apocalypse* belongs to no particular period: Iôannês had evidently acquired the language mainly by reading, picking up his vocabulary largely from ancient works, or else lived in some community in Asia Minor where the language was preserved in its older form. Thus he invariably uses the word *polemos* for "battle" or mere personal combat, although in his day the word had taken the broader meaning of "war," and *machê* was the usual word for "battle." War, in the sense of protracted hostilities, is not mentioned in the *Apocalypse,* which in every instance speaks only of a brief conflict, told in very few words, or of mere combats between two individuals. The battle between Mikael and the Dragon, with their respective hosts, resulting in the expulsion of the evil serpent from the sky, allegorizes the exclusion from the mind of all impure thoughts, especially those relating to the subject of sex. For Satan, the red Divinity, stands for nothing more or less than the principle of Desire in all its innumerable gradations, from the vaguest yearnings and the mere promptings of the appetites of the body down to the grossest phases of passion and lust; and all of these have their source in the instinct of reproduction, the attracting and cohering force of generated life. The creative Logos is the Dragon of Light, or Day-Sun; and Satan, the Adversary, is the Dragon of Darkness, or Night-Sun.

Very little is said in the *Apocalypse* concerning the psychic body; in fact, it is almost ignored, being tacitly included in the mortal, generated nature. While the spiritual awakening is necessarily accompanied by more or less psychic development, the latter may proceed independently of, and even adversely to, the true noetic progress; and the pursuit of psychism for its own sake leads inevitably to moral death. The psychic consciousness should not be dragged down into, and confused with, the normal consciousness on the physical plane of life; for the psychological result of thus confounding the two worlds is simply ordinary insanity, differing from common lunacy only in that it is suicidally self-inflicted, and therefore in the highest degree culpable, instead of being merely a misfortune caused by mental disease. The psychic body has its own place, in its own world, and is chiefly of importance after the death of the physical form—hence the encomium, "they did not esteem their psychic bodies until death." As Iôannês says in his *Evangel* (xii. 25), "He who loves his psychic body will lose it; and he who disregards his psychic body in this world will preserve it for [its] cyclic (*aiônion*) life." In Apocalyptic symbolism the psychic (lunar) body would be the bride of the Beast, as the solar body is the bride of the Lamb. In fact, an ancient reading of ii. 20 has "your wife Iezabêl."

CH. XII. 13–17

When the Dragon saw that he was hurled down to the earth, he kept pursuing the Woman who gave birth to the man-child. The Woman was endowed with the great Eagle's two wings, so that she might fly to the desert, to her place, where she is being nourished for a season, and seasons, and half a season, from the face of the Snake. The Snake spouted water after the Woman, like a river, that he might cause her to be carried away by the torrent. The earth rescued the Woman: the earth opened her mouth and swallowed up the river which the Dragon spouted from his mouth. The Dragon waxed passionate over the Woman, and went away to battle with the rest of her seed, who keep the commands of the God and have the evidence of the Anointed Iêsous; and he stationed himself on the sand of the sea.

COMMENTARY

The Virgin Mother being *sushumnâ*, the two wings of the Eagle are *îdâ* and *pingala*. The winged Woman represents the objective, or substantial, working of the *kundalinî*, while the three witnesses answer to its subjective, or noetic, aspect.

Foiled in his designs on the man-child (the nascent solar body), the Dragon seeks to arrest the spiritual growth of the neophyte by pouring out a flood of psychic phenomenal illusions, but the force thus engendered is absorbed by the material nature; and then, stationing himself on the margin of the sea (the finer and more æsthetic elements of the epithumetic principle), he combats the intuitions of the intellectual nature. Astronomically, the river spouted out by the Dragon is Eridanus, a winding constellation in the southern hemisphere, also called the River of Orion, which, when Virgo is in ascension, is setting and therefore apparently being swallowed by the earth.

The phrase "season, and seasons, and half a season," is only a puzzling variant of the forty-two months and the 1260 days, namely, three and a half years.

CHAPTER XIII. 1–4

I saw rising out of the sea a [constellatory] Beast, having ten horns and seven heads, and on his horns ten diadems, and on his heads [seven] names of profanities. The Beast which I saw was like a leopard, his feet were like a bear's [feet], and his mouth was like a lion's mouth. The Dragon gave him his force and his throne, and great authority. I saw one of his heads [drooping] as if it had been slain in the Death[-world]; but his death-blow was healed. The whole earth became admiring followers of the Beast. They also worshipped the Dragon because he gave authority to the Beast, and they worshipped the Beast, saying:

"Who is a match for the Beast? Is any one strong enough to meet him in combat?"

COMMENTARY

In stellar symbolism the Beast is the constellation now called Cetus, which is represented, however, not as a Whale but as a nondescript marine monster. The Arabians and the Jews called it the Sea-Lion; and it was also named the Leopard and the Sea-Bear. Iôannês has combined these various representations of it, presenting a composite picture. As a caricature of the psycho-material mind, the original figure, in the form drawn by the ancients who invented the zodiacal language, would seem to be sufficiently grotesque, but Iôannês has given it additional touches of satire. The Beast is said to rise from the sea and to receive power from the Dragon, because it is the product of the two lower planes, the psychic and the material; its seven heads are the seven ruling epithumetic desires, each of which is a profanation of the Divine Desire; its ten horns are the five intellectual faculties doubled, because its every faculty is dual and at war with itself; the horns are all adorned with diadems to indicate the false pride of the lower intellect. As this lower mind is the shadow or reflected image, so to say, of the true mind, the Nous, which is symbolized as the Lion, the Beast is pictured as a Pseudo-Lion, a hybrid, for it resembles the Leopard, which was fabled to be a cross between the Lion (*leo*) and the Panther (*pardus*);

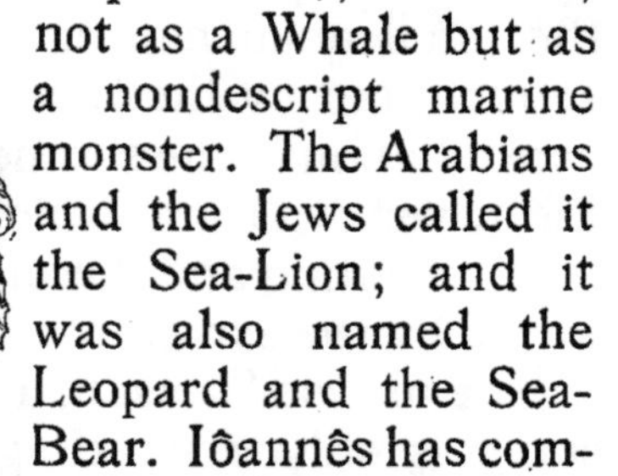
Cetus

it is slow-going, with the ponderous paws of the Bear, and has a mouth like a Lion, thus simulating the voice of the Nous. It represents the highest development of the human intellect dissociated from philosophic reason and spiritual intuition, and it is indeed the admiration of the whole world of the profane. The head that is seemingly slain and yet resurrects is the desire for life on the plane of the senses, a desire which the neophyte must utterly eradicate. In a more general sense, the lower mind, whenever it attempts philosophy, is never quite certain that life is worth living; and in its utter blindness to spiritual realities, perceiving only the phenomena of the material world, it formulates theories of existence based merely upon them, regarding all else as unknowable.

CH. XIII. 5–10

There was given him a mouth speaking great [boastings] and profanities; and authority was given him to do [this] for forty-two months. He opened his mouth in profanity against the God, to profane his name, his tent, and those pitching tent in the sky. It was given him to do battle with the devotees, and to conquer them; and authority was given him over every tribe, nation, tongue and people. All those who dwell on the earth will worship him—[every one] whose name has not been registered in the sacrificed Lamb's scroll of life since the evolution of the world. If any one has an ear, let him hear: If any one welcomes captivity, into captivity he goes; if any one shall kill with the sword, with the sword must he be killed. Here is the patience and the faith of the devotees.

COMMENTARY

In this allegorical exposition of the powers and peculiarities of the lower mind-principle, only part applies to the particular case of the Conqueror, the rest being of a general nature; for without this broader application the treatment of the subject would necessarily be incomplete and obscure. Thus the forty-two months (three and a half years) refers to the first half of the seven-year initiatory cycle, during which the neophyte, passing through the psychic stages of his development, and thereby intensifying the action of the psycho-phrênic mind, has to struggle constantly against its influence; but the rest of the explanatory matter relates to mankind in general.

Those who have not been registered in the book of life (see also ch. xvii. 8) are the great majority who have not in any incarnation, during the cycle of material evolution, attained the noetic consciousness. For, once a man has even glimpsed the supernal truths, he can never again rest content with the illusory images of the material world or worship at the shrine of mere intellectualism; the true Self, the Master-Mind, has placed his seal upon him, and he is thenceforth individualized from the irresponsible mass of mankind, and enrolled among those who must by an irresistible impulse, the call of the God, tread the path of man's higher destiny.

The word *katabolê,* here translated "evolution," is said by Origen to mean the descent of the souls into material conditions.

The formula, "He who has an ear, let him hear," is used by Iôannês as an appeal to the intuition. Here he states a broad principle: the man who craves material life by that very desire condemns himself to remain in the bondage of reincarnation and subject to the iron law of retribution which obtains in the lower spheres of existence. But the esotericist, knowing that nothing binds him to the physical form of life except the longings of his own heart, patiently endures all the ills of life, in full assurance that through the purification of his moral character he will attain deliverance.

CH. XIII. 11, 12

I saw another [constellatory] Beast rising out of the earth. He had two horns like a lamb, and he talked like a dragon. He is wielding all the authority of the first Beast in his presence, and he is causing the earth and all its inhabitants to worship the first Beast, whose death-blow was healed.

COMMENTARY

This Pseudo-Lamb is the dual sex-nature, the two riders of the dun horse in a different impersonation. He is the image on the material plane of the Lamb, who in the opening of the seven seals played the part of the rider of the white horse. Thus the Lamb and the Pseudo-Lamb bear the same relation to each other as do *Erôs,* the Divine Love, and *pothos* (Cupid), carnal love, not, however, as the base passion, but in its more refined forms as sentimental yearning, religious fervor of the irrational sort, and all the emotional impulses. He talks like a dragon, because from this source originate religious cant, sentimental ethics, and erotic utterances generally; and he has all the potentialities of the first Beast, the phrênic nature, for unutterable vileness. As a constellation, he is the Head of Medusa, the mortal Gorgon, called by the Jews *Rosch hasatan,* "Satan's Head." Owing to its proximity to Aries, this constellation was sometimes pictured wearing the two horns of the Ram, the Apocalyptic Lamb.

Medusa

CH. XIII. 13–18

He makes great omens, so that he may even make fire come down out of the sky to the earth in the sight of men. He keeps deluding those who dwell on the earth, through the omens which he was permitted to make in sight of the Beast, saying to those who dwell on the earth that they should make an image to the Beast who has the stroke of the sword and came to life. It was permitted [him] to bestow breath on it—the image of the Beast—so that the image of the Beast should not only talk but also cause that all [men] who might not worship the image of the Beast should be slain. He causes all [men], the small and the great, the rich and the poor, alike the freemen and the slaves, to be given a brand on their right hand or on their forehead, and that no one should be able to buy or to sell unless he has the brand—the name of the Beast, or the number of his name. Here is cleverness: let him who has the intuitive mind compute the number of the Beast; for it is the number of a man, and his number is six hundred and sixty-six.

COMMENTARY

Magical powers were attributed to Medusa, and talismans were made under its stellar influence. The word *sêmeion,* here translated "omen," signifies also a "talisman" or symbol drawn under the influence of some particular constellation or planetary aspect. Cedrenus states (p. 22) that Perseus (the slayer of the Gorgon) taught the Persians the magic of Medusa, by means of which fire came down out of the sky. But, apart from all exoteric notions of ceremonial magic, the Pseudo-Lamb of the *Apocalypse,* as a principle in man, does indeed draw down "fire" from the intellectual sky; for the force which it represents produces all the grosser forms of psychism, and is the agent of the so-called "miracles" of exoteric religion, the prodigies produced by erotic fervor, blind credulity and disordered imagination; and it is likewise the foul force employed in phallic sorcery. It is also the irrational instinct of religionism, the vague yearning for something to worship—a reflection or shadow of the true devotional principle—which prompts men to project a subjective image of the lower, personal mind, and to endow it with human attributes, and then to claim to receive "revelations" from it; and this—the image of the Beast, or unspiritual mind,—is their anthropomorphic God, a fabulous monster the worship of which has ever prompted men to fanaticism and persecution, and has inflicted untold misery and dread upon the masses of mankind, as well as physical torture and death in hideous forms upon the many martyrs who have refused to bend the knee to this Gorgonean phantom of the beast-mind of man. Truly, where the worshippers of this image of the Beast predominate, the man whose brow and hand are unbranded by this superstition, who neither thinks nor acts in accordance with it, suffers ostracism if not virulent persecution.

"Here is cleverness" would be, in the English idiom, "Here is a puzzle." The number of the Beast, as already explained, is simply *hê phrên,* the letters of which, as numerals, total 666; while the Pseudo-Lamb is *akrasia,* or 333.

CHAPTER XIV. 1–5

I saw; and, Behold! the Lamb standing on the mountain of Sion, and with him the one hundred and forty-four thousand having his name and his father's name written on their foreheads. I heard a voice from the sky, like the voice of many waters, like the voice of a great thunder; and the voice which I heard was like [that] of lyrists playing on their lyres. They chanted as it were a new lyric before the throne, and before the four Beings and the Ancients, and no one could understand the lyric save the hundred and forty-four thousand—they who had been bought from the earth. These are the ones who were not defiled with women; for they are virgins. These are the ones who go along with the Lamb wherever he goes. These were bought from men—a firstling to the God and the Lamb. In their mouth was found no deceit; they are faultless.

COMMENTARY

The Lamb is the fourth of the animal-symbols, or "beasts," and is identical with the Bowman on the white horse, the regent of the fourth somatic division. He is the intellectual Sun, the Nous, which is Iêsous, the number of whose name is 888. The Sun is the Lion when domiciled in Leo, which corresponds to the highest of the noetic *chakras*, and the Lamb when exalted

Agnus Dei

in Aries, which corresponds to the nimbus; and his being on Sion's hill also signifies that exaltation. Here he is represented as being surrounded by his virginal powers, and a thunderous chorus preludes the next act in the drama, the conquest of the cardiac centres. But this chorus, the fifth in the series, is only described, no words being given because, it is intimated, it would be unintelligible to the profane; and the conquest of the *chakras* of this division is given with less detail than are the others.

CH. XIV. 6, 7

I saw another Divinity flying in mid-sky, having an æonian divine message to announce to those seated on the earth, to every people, tribe, tongue and nation, and he said with a loud voice:

"Fear ye the God and to him give glory; for the hour of his judgment is come! Worship him who made the sky, the earth, the sea and the springs of waters."

COMMENTARY

This, the third of the conquests, is represented as a harvesting of the intellectual, psychic and spiritual principles, to which correspond respectively the cerebro-spinal axis, the great sympathetic nervous system, and the aureola. The action is therefore confined to the three higher centres corresponding to these principles; while the opening of the four lower centres is given as a proclamation to each of the four lower principles seated in the somatic divisions.

An æon (*aiôn*) is a definite life-period, as the life-time of a man, a generation, or the whole evolutionary period, the complete cycle of generation. It is only the crude, unphilosophical notion that eternity is "a long period of time" that has caused the "authorized" translators of the *New Testament* to persist in giving *aiônios* the meaning "eternal." Time is not an entity or a thing *per se*, nor is eternity merely time indefinitely prolonged. Time is only a mental concept arising from the consciousness of change in the phenomenal world; whereas eternity is noumenal, changeless, extending neither into the "past" nor the "future," and therefore is an immeasurable "present."

The æonian evangel relates only to the cycle of generation—from which the hero of the Apocalyptic drama, the Conqueror, is about to be emancipated, after final judgment has been passed upon his deeds during the æon, in which he has been successively incarnated among all the races and peoples who have had their lesser cycles in the vast period of human evolution.

CH. XIV. 8

Another, a second Divinity, came after [him], saying:

"She fell! Babylon the great fell—she who has made all the people drink of the wine of the lust of her prostitution!"

COMMENTARY

Babylon, elsewhere called the Woman in scarlet, personifies the physical nature, the carnal body and the lust for existence inherent in its elements. It has "fallen" only in the sense that the consciousness of the Conqueror has become free from its trammels.

CH. XIV. 9–13

Another Divinity, the third, came after them, saying with a great voice:

"If any one worships the Beast and his image, and receives a brand on his forehead or on his [right] hand, *he* also shall drink of the wine of the God's ardor which has been poured out raw into the wine-cup of his passion; and he shall be tormented with fire and sulphur in presence of the holy Divinities and in presence of the Lamb. The smoke of their torment keeps going up throughout æons of æons, and no rest day or night are they having who worship the Beast and his image, and whosoever receives the brand of his name. Here is the patience of the devotees, those who are keeping the commands of the God and the belief of Iêsous."

I heard a voice from the sky, saying:

"Write: Immortal are 'the dead' who die in the Master henceforth. 'Yea,' says the Breath, 'that they may cease from their *labors*—but their *works* accompany them.' "

COMMENTARY

The creative Breath, which at its deific source is the supernal Love, becomes, in the spheres of generation, the force which engenders bodies, and in that respect the worshippers of the Beast and his image, the personal God, partake of it, and thereby are constantly undergoing the miseries of embodied existence, in which they find no abiding peace. Yet physical existence is in reality a purificatory discipline, like the fumigating with sulphur (a common practice with the ancients) alluded to by Iôannês. The followers of Iêsous, the spiritual Mind, knowing this, endure life with patience and faith in the divine justice. The "dead" are the *living dead*, the embodied souls, who "die in the Master" only when they attain liberation from the sepulchre of the carnal body, ceasing then from their toil but retaining the fruition of their good works.

CH. XIV. 14–16

I saw; and, Behold! a white cloud; and on the cloud [I saw] sitting [a Divinity] like the son of man, having on his head a golden crown, and in his hand a keen sickle.

Another Divinity came out from the adytum, crying out with a loud voice to the [Divinity] seated on the cloud:

"Thrust out your sickle and reap, for to you has come the hour to reap—for the earth's harvest is dried up."

The [Divinity] seated on the cloud struck his sickle on the earth, and the earth was reaped.

COMMENTARY

The fifth Divinity represents the First Logos, here seated in the nimbus; for he is the overshadowing Self, the Uncrucified, or unincarnated. He reaps the scant harvest of the psychic nature. It will be noticed that wherever he is referred to in this passage the word "Divinity" (*angelos*) has been expunged from the text, apparently by some zealot who, recognizing the description as that of the Christos, tampered with the manuscript with the same motive, presumably, which prompts the modern "orthodox" translators to shade misleadingly the values of the Greek tenses, in very many instances.

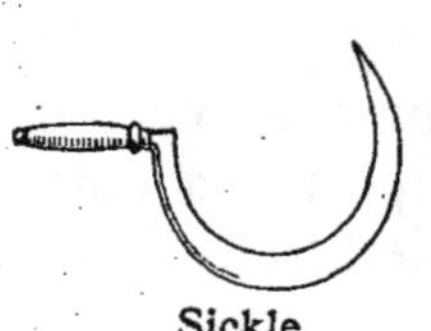
Sickle

CH. XIV. 17–20

Came from the adytum which is in the sky another Divinity, he also having a keen sickle.

Another Divinity came out from the altar—he who has authority over fire—and he gave voice with a great shout to the one who had the keen sickle, saying:

"Thrust out your keen sickle and pick the grape-clusters of the earth's vine, for her bunches of grapes are ripened."

The Divinity struck his sickle into the earth and stripped the earth's vine, and threw [the grapes] into the wine-vat, the great [womb] of the God's ardor. The wine-vat was trodden outside the city, and blood issued from the wine-vat, up to the bridles of the horses, as far as one thousand and six hundred *stadia*.

COMMENTARY

The second of the two Reapers is the Second Logos, and he reaps the spiritually dynamic nature, which on the plane of creative forces corresponds to the fivefold noetic group. The "vine" of this conquest is identical with the "river Euphrates" of the three other conquests. Physiologically, it is the spinal cord, the path of the five *prânas*, or life-winds, which are now, by the exigencies of the allegory, metamorphosed into bunches of grapes. These solar forces, permeating and energizing the aura (the wine-vat *outside* the city), produce a return current to the *chakras* of the four somatic divisions (the *bridles* of the horses) and into the solar body, the 1,600, or *to sôma hêliakon.* It is a process analogous to the nutrition of the fœtus *in utero.*

In stellar symbolism, each of these seven Divinities may be recognized among the constellations. Thus, for instance, as Aries, the Sion of the allegory, rises in the eastern horizon, the Eagle is near the zenith, together with the Swan and the Celestial Vulture, these being the three Divinities who are said to fly in the mid-sky.

CHAPTER XV. 1–4

I saw another constellation in the sky, great and wonderful, [and in it] seven Divinities having the seven scourges, the final [ordeals], for by them the God's ardor is finished.

I saw [a sheen], as it were a glassy sea, mixed with fire, and those who were Conquerors of the Beast, of his image, and of the number of his name, standing on the glassy sea, having lyres of the God. They keep chanting the lyric of Moses, a slave of the God, and the lyric of the Lamb, saying:

"Great and wonderful are thy works, O Master-God, the All-Dominator. Just and true are thy paths, thou Ruler of the Æons. Who shall not fear, O Master, and glorify thy name? For thou art the Only Sanctified. For all the people shall come and worship before thee. For thy just deeds have been made manifest."

COMMENTARY

This constellation is Taurus, and the seven Divinities answer to the Pleiades, the group of stars situated in the neck of the stellar Bull, who is the symbol of *spiritual* generative force.

In the *Old Testament* mythology, Moses represented the Sun in Aries. His pæan of victory after crossing the Red Sea (*Ex.* xiv. 26–31; xv. 1–21) is presumably the one here referred to; for the Red

Sea stood for the sea of generation. The crystalline and fiery sea is the celestial ether.

CH. XV. 5–8; XVI. 1

After these [things] I saw; and, Behold! the adytum of the tent-temple of the evidence in the sky was opened. Came out from the adytum the seven Divinities having the seven scourges, clothed in flawless and brilliant [diamond-]stone, and girded about their breasts with golden girdles. One of the four Beings gave the seven Divinities seven golden libation-saucers full of the ardor of the God who lives throughout the æons of the æons. The adytum was filled with smoke from the glory of the God and from his inherent force, and no one was able to go into the adytum until the seven scourges of the seven Divinities should be finished. I heard a great voice from the adytum, saying to the seven Divinities:

"Go and pour out into the earth the seven libation-saucers of the God's ardor."

COMMENTARY

The seven superlatively pure and dazzling Divinities who emerge from the "most holy place" of the tabernacle are, like the Planetary Logos whose apparition is described in the opening vision, androgynous: each is a male figure with female breasts and wearing the girdle of Aphroditê. Here, however, the word *stêthê* is used, which is applicable to either sex, while in the other instance the word is *mastoi,* which applies more particularly to the female breasts. The *hermaphroditos,* or blended figure of Hermês (Mercury) and Aphroditê (Venus), was a familiar figure in Greek art. In both the Greek and the Jewish mystery-paraphernalia the "ark" contained the male and female emblems. As the Planetary Logos is inverted, mirrored upside-down in the material world, these seven androgynous Divinities, although they have to do with the lowest of the somatic divisions, are yet the highest and purest of all. They are the finishers of the great work of regeneration, and the precursors of the Conqueror on the white horse. Each has a *phialê,* a shallow cup, or saucer, used in pouring out drink-offerings to the Gods, and the libations they pour out consist of the primordial creative force-substance — the ether. This ether, as symbolized by the diamond-glittering raiment of the seven Divinities, is colorless and without qualities of its own; but all qualities are imparted to it by the Thought of the God. As Paracelsus says, "All things when they come from the hand of God are white; he colors them afterward according to his pleasure."

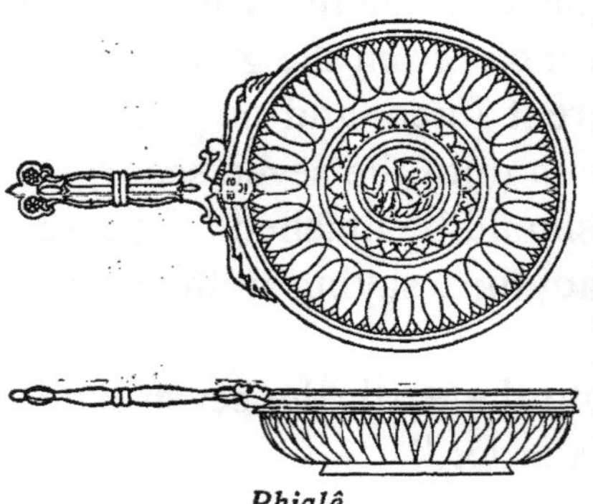

Phialê

CHAPTER XVI. 2

The first [Divinity] went and poured out his libation-saucer into the earth. There came to be a bad and painful sore on the men who had the brand of the Beast, and who worshipped his image.

COMMENTARY

The earth, or lowest division, is the throne of the Pseudo-Seer; and the worshippers of the Beast and his image are the forms of thought mirrored in this lowest reflector of the noetic consciousness, where they become distorted into the crude elemental notions of religion. These are represented as ulcerating; for the time has come for the complete eradication of the centres whence they radiate.

CH. XVI. 3

The second Divinity poured out his libation-saucer into the sea. It became blood like a dead man's, and every psychic form of life in the sea died.

COMMENTARY

The sea, or umbilical centre, is the throne of the Dragon, the epithumetic, lower psychic nature. The libation eliminates from it the last vestiges of the passions and desires; and the aura of this division is suffused by the golden, orange-yellow color of the *prânas*.

Ch. xvi. 4–7

The third Divinity poured out his libation-saucer into the rivers and the springs of the waters, and the [waters] became blood. I heard the Divinity of the waters saying:

"Thou art just, O Master, [thou] who [for ever] *art*, who wast, and who art sanctified; for thou didst pass this sentence upon [the followers of the Beast]: for they poured out the blood of devotees and seers, and blood thou hast given them to drink; for they are deserving [of it]."

I heard [the Divinity hovering above] the altar saying:

"Verily, O Master-God, the All-Dominator, true and just are thy judgments!"

COMMENTARY

The rivers and springs are the throne of the Beast; it receives the golden color when the solar force reaches it. Its regent is the phrênic mind, which distorts and falsifies the intuitions reaching it from the noetic faculty. The Divinity of the waters is the *Zôon* corresponding to this centre, and the one hovering over the altar (ch. viii. 3) is the *Zôon* of the noetic centre.

Here the word "coming," in the formula applied to the God, is replaced by "sanctified"; for now the God has come, the future being merged in the present.

CH. XVI. 8, 9

The fourth Divinity poured out his libation-saucer upon the sun. [Authority] was given it to scorch men with fire. Men were scorched with great heat, and they profaned the name of the God who has authority over these scourges; but they did not reform to give him glory.

COMMENTARY

The Sun is the throne of the Sky-God, the Lion. The outpouring of the *speirêma* upon this centre produces intense mental strain. The intellectual forces are represented as unrepentant and profane, simply because the Nous, undifferentiated Thought, is the "only sanctified."

CH. XVI. 10, 11

The fifth Divinity poured out his libation-saucer upon the throne of the Beast. His realm became darkened; and his [subjects] gnawed their tongues for pain, and profaned the God of the sky because of their pains and sores; but they did not reform from their works.

COMMENTARY

The Beast's throne, as a somatic division, is the cardiac centre; but in a general way it includes the whole sympathetic system, of which the principal *chakra*, the epigastric plexus, is shared by the Dragon.

CH. XVI. 12

The sixth Divinity poured out his libation-saucer upon that great river, the Euphrates. Its waters were dried up, so that there might be prepared the path of the rulers who [come out] from the birthplace of the sun.

COMMENTARY

In each of the four conquests the sixth *chakra* is related to the cerebro-spinal axis and the five *prânas*, the solar or noetic forces, since the forces act on each of the four planes of existence, to which the somatic divisions correspond. In this final conquest the waters of the Euphrates, that is, the magnetic or nerve-force of the spinal system, are dried up; for henceforth the solar electric fires are to take their place permanently. In the "sacred city," the solar body, the Euphrates becomes the main-street, or thoroughfare, "of pure gold, transparent as glass."

CH. XVI. 13–16

I saw [coming] out of the mouth of the Dragon, out of the mouth of the Beast, and out of the mouth of the Pseudo-Seer, three unpurified spirits, like frogs. For they are spirits of spectres, making omens, [and] they are going out among the rulers of the whole home-land, to muster them for the battle of the great day [of the coming] of the God, the All-Dominator. [The God says:]

"Behold! I am coming [silently], like a thief. Immortal is he who stays awake and keeps on his outer garments, so that he may not walk naked, and they see his shame."

They mustered them in the place which is called in Hebrew *Harmagedôn.*

COMMENTARY

The forces expelled by the drying up of the "Euphrates" issue from the three lower somatic centres and form a psychic entity analogous to the ghost of a deceased person: the after-death process of purification undergone by the soul takes place before death in him who "dies in the Master." The soul of the disincarnated man, before entering upon its period of blissful rest in the higher world-soul, the spiritual realm, has to purge itself of all the evil forces and elements of the psychic nature; and these discarded elements remain in the lower world-soul, the phantasmal realm, where they constitute, for a time, a psychic entity wearing the semblance of the departed personality, its ghost, shade or spectre—an elemental self, which is a congeries of all the impure and evil constituents thus rejected by the soul. In Greek mysticism, as expounded by Plotinos and others, this higher world-soul was termed Zeus, and the lower world-soul, which is next to the material realm and is rendered foul by the impure emanations from the latter, was called Rhea; the latter stands for the Kabalistic "astral light," which is kinetically charged with the evil impulses and thoughts of humanity, and especially with the foul sexuality of the depraved portion of mankind, and by its hypnotic influence is a constant inciter to crime and vice. In this realm the spectre gradually disintegrates; but the elements composing it are again attracted to the soul when it reincarnates. But in the case of the individual who is engaged in the telestic work this elemental self becomes a malignant demon, against which he must constantly be on his guard, and which he must eventually destroy. The impure "spirits" (*pneumata*) are said to congregate in the place called *Harmagedôn*. The scholiasts have failed to find even a plausible Hebrew derivation for this word; the supposition that it stands for "Mount Megiddo" meets with the difficulty that the only Megiddo known to geography was a city on a plain. Considered as an anagram, *Harmagedôn* forms *Rhea 'dagmôn*, "Rhea of the prurient itchings, or desires"—a very accurate characterization of the *anima bruta*, or brute-soul of the world, which Rhea typified. The worship of the Goddess Rhea, who was called also Cybêle, Astartê, and by many other names and titles, was wide-spread among oriental nations. Her numerous temples abounded in "consecrated women," and as the *Magna Mater*, "the Great Mother" of these prostitutes, she was worshipped with shameless orgiastic rites. Originally, however, Rhea symbolized the celestial ether.

CH. XVI. 17–21

The seventh Divinity poured out his libation-saucer into the air. There came a great voice from the adytum of the sky—from the throne—saying: "He has been born!"

There came to be voices, lightnings and thunders; and there came to be a great earthquake, such as has not happened since men were born upon the earth—such and so great an earthquake.

The great city came to be in three divisions. The cities of the people fell; and Babylon the great was remembered before the God, to give to her the wine-cup of the wine of the ardor of his passion. Every island fled, and the mountains were not found. Great hail, like hundred-pound [catapult missiles], keeps coming down from the sky upon men, and men profaned the God because of the scourge of the hail; for its scourge is exceedingly great.

COMMENTARY

The voice from the adytum, that of the First Logos, announces the birth "from above" of the Conqueror, who thereupon appears on the white horse; but before this apparition is described a digression is made, to introduce explanatory matter.

The great city, the physical body, is now three-divisional, the minor cities, the procreative centres, having been extirpated.

CHAPTER XVII. 1–5

Came one of the seven Divinities who had the seven libation-saucers, and talked with me, saying:

"Hither! I shall show you the judgment of the great prostitute who is sitting on the many waters, with whom the rulers of the earth committed fornication—and those who dwell on the earth became intoxicated with the wine of her prostitution."

He carried me away in the Breath[-trance] into the desert; and I saw a Woman sitting on a scarlet Beast, [having his mouth] full of names of profanity, and having seven heads and ten horns. The Woman was arrayed in purple and scarlet, overjewelled with gold, precious stone and pearls, having in her hand a golden wine-cup, full of the stenches and filth of her prostitution. On her forehead was a name written:

"A Mystery: Babylon the great, the 'Mother' of the [temple-]prostitutes and of the earth's stenches."

COMMENTARY

The two "Women" of the *Apocalypse* are both "Goddesses," in the pagan sense, precisely as the "Angels" are the lesser Gods of the pagan pantheon; and, whether Christian or pagan, all these Gods and Goddesses are the personified powers and principles of the macrocosm and the microcosm. Babylon, as the "mighty city," is the human body; and as the fallen Woman she is a Goddess, the *Magna Mater* of the temple prostitutes in the Mystery-cult of Rhea, or Astartê.

Babylon, the human body, is a Mystery, truly. The anatomists, physiologists, surgeons and physicians, who have studied this Mystery even on a strictly empirical and materialistic basis, have gained more knowledge of the divine Life manifested in the material world, and have conferred vastly greater benefits on the human race, than have all the exoteric religionists who have wasted their lives in formulating fantastic theologies and in coercing their fellow-men into the worship of that figment of the unenlightened mind—the personal God. But Babylon represents more than the physical body considered as a mere form composed of various tissues, a congeries of functional organs: it symbolizes also the broad principle of generation, of life confined to a physical basis. According to the arcane science, which Iôannês has outlined in allegorical language, forces are subtile elements, and the material elements are forces that have grown inert; and all the forces and elements have their origin in the celestial ether, the Archê, or "first principle." The Sun-clothed Virgin of the Sky, who gives birth to the man-child, by the gestation of the solar body of the Conqueror, is the pure ether, the primordial force-substance; but in the spheres of animal-human generation, where that ether has become differentiated into the gross material elements, she is the unchaste female, the mother of all that is abominable. As an external form, a marvellous organism evolved by the soul for its own divine purposes, the body is the adytum of the God; but the elements composing it have become foul during the long ages of material evolution, so that the soul is ever being tainted and instigated to evil by the impure emanations and vicious impulses which have become inherent in the physical organism. It is thus a Mystery at once divine and infernal, at which the seer represents himself as gazing in wonder.

Crater

As a Goddess, the infernal Aphroditê, the depraved Virgo symbolizes the *anima bruta,* or lower world-soul, which is saturated with sexuality. In this rôle she holds a cup, which is the adjacent constellation Crater, the Mixing-bowl fabled to have belonged to Iacchos, the God of orgiastic revelry.

CH. XVII. 6–8

I saw the Woman intoxicated with the blood of the devotees and with the blood of the witnesses of

Iêsous. When I saw her, I gazed in wonderment, with great curiosity. Said the Divinity to me:

"Why did you wonder? I shall tell you the mystery of the Woman, and of the Beast that was carrying her, which has the seven heads and the ten horns. The Beast which you saw *was*, and *is* not, and is about to come up out of the abyss and go to destruction. Those who dwell on the earth—[the men] whose name has not been registered on the scroll of life since the evolution of the world—will wonder when they look at the Beast, because he *was*, and *is* not, and shall be present!

COMMENTARY

The red Dragon, the epithumetic, passional nature, is the principle which, in close alliance with the Beast, or phrênic mind, impels the soul to continue to incarnate, and he thus sustains the Woman, who typifies physical existence. He rises from the abyss, the impure elements, and is again disintegrated in them when the soul is purified. The formula, "*was, is* not and shall be present," merely expresses in an enigmatical way the Platonic doctrine that in the spheres of generation "nothing really *is*, but all things are becoming"; that is, in the phenomenal world nothing partakes of permanent being, but "all things are being created and destroyed, coming into existence and passing into new forms." The men who have not been registered on the scroll of life are simply the uninitiated.

CH. XVII. 9–11

"Here is the intuitive mind that has cleverness: the seven heads are seven mountains where the Woman is sitting on them; and they are seven rulers, [of whom] the five have fallen, and the one *is*, and the other has not yet come, and when he does come he must abide a little while. The Beast which *was* and *is* not, is himself also an eighth and is [an emanation] from the seven—and to destruction he is going.

COMMENTARY

The seven heads of the Dragon are, like those of the Beast, the seven cardinal desires, but in the one they are mental, in the other instinctual; and the seven mountains are the seven *chakras* through which they manifest during incarnation (the Woman being then seated on them), and they dominate in turn the seven incarnations through which the neophyte must pass in conquering them. The irreclaimable residue of the epithumetic principle, which goes to form the after-death spectre, or elemental self, is the eighth, "the son of perdition." The Conqueror is represented in the Apocalyptic drama as being in the sixth of the series of seven incarnations, so that five of them have perished and the seventh is yet to come; hence the Dragon, later on in the drama, is again imprisoned in the abyss, and can not be utterly slain until that seventh and last incarnation.

CH. XVII. 12–14

"The ten horns which you saw are ten rulers who have not yet received a realm; but they receive authority as rulers one hour with the Beast. These have one purpose; and their force and authority they pass along to the Beast. These will battle with the Lamb, and the Lamb will conquer them; for he is Master of masters and Ruler of rulers; and those who [go along] with him are called and chosen and reliable."

COMMENTARY

The ten horns are the five *prânas*, each of which is dual, positive and negative, on this plane, where they are merely the life-winds, or vital forces; they are not related to the *chakras* as the *tattvas* are, and hence are said to have no realm as yet, though later they have the spinal axis for their realm, when the Lamb has conquered them. Exuberant animal vitality, by intensifying the passional nature, tends away from spirituality; hence these forces are represented as being inimical to the Nous, yet they are to be conquered and utilized. The forces subdued are here classified according to the three lower degrees of initiation in the Christian secret society.

CH. XVII. 15–18

Also he says to me:

"The waters which you saw, where the prostitute is sitting, are nations, mobs, peoples and tongues.

The ten horns which you saw on the Beast—these shall abhor the prostitute and shall make her destitute and naked, and shall devour her flesh and consume her with fire. For the God put it in their hearts to carry out his purpose, to carry [it] out [as their own] one purpose, and to give their realm to the Beast until the instruction of the God should be finished. And the Woman whom you saw is the great city which has a realm [extending] over the rulers of the earth."

COMMENTARY

The waters are the great sea of generated life, humanity in its vast cycle of material and psychic evolution, which comprises all lesser racial and subracial cycles, in each of which every individual plays his part; and the whole mighty tide of life slowly works out the divine purpose. Even the minor forces of the individual man have in them the impulse of this purpose of the God, so that he who runs counter to it invites disease and destruction from the very forces that normally vitalize his physical form. The "rulers of the earth" are the underlying forces of the material world.

CHAPTER XVIII. 1–3

After these [instructions] I saw another Divinity coming down out of the sky, having great authority; and the earth was lit up by his glory. He cried out with a strong voice, saying:

"She fell! The great Babylon fell, and became a haunt of ghosts, a prison of every filthy spectre and a cage of every filthy and loathesome bird [of prey.] For by the wine of the lust of her prostitution all the people have fallen. The rulers of the earth committed fornication with her; and the merchants of the earth by the force of her lewdness grew rich."

COMMENTARY

The Apocalyptic hero, having conquered in the ordeals of his initiation, achieving the spiritual rebirth, has risen above the illusions of life, and has taken his place among the deathless Gods. The exhortations and lamentations which follow the declaration of the radiant Divinity concerning the fall of Babylon are of a general nature, applying to the aggregate of humanity, and not at all to the Conqueror. For, as there are two crucifixions, so there are, correspondingly, two falls. The fall of Babylon referred to by the Divinity is the fall into mortal corruption, the desecration by humanity of their physical bodies, which they have converted into holds of iniquity. But, as pertaining to the Conqueror, the fall of Babylon is the exact reverse of this; for it means the conquest, subjugation and purification of the body.

The people, rulers and merchants who were debauched by the great prostitute are the three lower castes—the toiling, combative and commercial classes—while the Divinities represent the fourth and highest class, the enlightened.

CH. XVIII. 4–24

I heard another voice from the sky, saying:

"Come out from her, O my people, so that you may not have partnership in her sins, and so that you may not receive of her scourges! For her sins have followed [you] up to the sky, and the God has held in memory her misdeeds. Pay her back as *she* also paid back, and double to her twofold [wages], according to her works. In the wine-cup which she poured out, pour out for her a double [draught]. As much as she glorified herself and grew lewd, so much give her of torment and mourning; for in her heart she keeps saying:

" 'I sit enthroned a queen, and am not a widow; and I shall not at all put on mourning.'

"Therefore in one day shall come her scourges—death, mourning and hunger—and she shall be consumed by fire. For strong is the Master-God who judged her. The rulers of the earth, who committed fornication and were lustful with her, shall weep and wail over her when they look at the smoke of her conflagration, standing afar through fear of her torment, saying:

" 'Woe! Woe! The great city, Babylon, the strong city! For in one hour has come your judgment!'

"The merchants of the earth shed tears and mourn over her, for no one buys their stock any more—the stock of gold, silver, precious stone, pearls, byssus, purple [cloth] and silken [fabrics]; and all citrus wood, every ivory utensil, every utensil [made] of very precious wood, of bronze, of iron and of marble; and cinnamon, amomum, incense, ointment, frankincense, wine, oil, flour, wheat, cattle and sheep; and [merchandise] of horses and chariots—*and of bodies and souls of men!* The fruits which your soul lusted for are gone from you, and all dainty and radiant [charms] have perished from you, and [your lovers] shall never more find them at all [in you]. The merchants of these wares, who were enriched by her, shall stand afar through fear of her torment, shedding tears and mourning, saying:

" 'Woe! Woe! The great city—she who was arrayed in byssus [fabric], purple and scarlet, and over-jewelled with gold, precious stone and pearl! For in one hour all this wealth has come to destitution.'

"And every sailing-master, and every crew on the ships, sailors, and as many as toil [on] the sea, stood afar and cried out, on seeing the smoke of her conflagration, saying:

" 'What [city] is the equal of the great city?'

"And they threw dust on their heads and cried out, weeping and sorrowing, saying:

" 'Woe! Woe! The great city, by whom all were enriched who have ships on the sea, from her bountifulness! For in one hour she has come to destitution.'

"Rejoice over her, O sky, and ye devotees, apostles and seers! For the God has passed sentence upon her in accordance with your decision."

A lone Divinity, the strong one, took up a stone, like a great millstone, and threw it into the sea, saying:

"Thus with a rush shall Babylon, the great city, be thrown down, and shall not at all be found any more. The voice of lyrists, musicians, flutists and trumpeters shall not at all be heard in thee any more; no craftsman, of whatever craft, shall be found any more at all in thee; the voice of a millstone shall not at all be heard in thee any more; the light of a lamp shall not at all shine in thee any more; and the voice of the bridegroom and of the bride shall not at all be heard in thee any more. For thy merchants were the magnates of the earth. For by thy witchcraft all the people were deluded."

In her was found the blood of seers and devotees, and of all who have been sacrificed on the earth.

COMMENTARY

In the rejoicing and lamentation over the prospective fall of Babylon (an event which, for the mass of mankind, lies in the extremely remote future) the four castes take part. The highest caste, or distinctive class, is given as threefold, composed of devotees, apostles and seers; but they utter no rejoicings, the Divinities acting as their spokesmen. The profane, comprising the rulers or dominant warlike class, the merchants or trading class, and the sailors, the toiling masses on the sea of life, indulge in lamentations over the downfall of the great city. For the present, and for ages to come, in Christian and pagan lands alike, Astartê remains enthroned on the scarlet Dragon, "who is the Devil and Satan," and in this twentieth century her cup is more overflowing with abominations, and the traffic in the bodies and souls of men and of women goes on even more briskly and heartlessly, than in the days when Iôannês penned his mystic scroll. The destruction of the Apocalyptic Babylon will come only when humanity shall have learned to loathe the lusts of the flesh and to love the glories of the spirit.

CHAPTER XIX. 1–8

After these [lamentations] I heard [a chorus], as it were the voice of a vast throng in the sky, saying:

"*Hallêlouia!* The deliverance, glory and force are our God's. For true and just are his judgments: for he has judged the great prostitute, who corrupted the earth with her prostitution, and he has avenged the blood of his slaves at her hand."

And once more they have said:

"*Hallêlouia!* Her smoke keeps going up throughout the æons of the æons!"

The twenty-four Ancients and the four Beings fell down and worshipped the God seated on the throne, saying:

"AMÊN. *Hallêlouia!*"

A voice came out of the throne, saying:

"Praise ye our God, all ye his slaves, and ye who fear him, both the small and the great."

And I heard [a chorus], as it were the voice of a vast throng, as the voice of many waters, and as the voice of mighty thunders, saying:

"*Hallêlouia!* For the Master-God, the All-Dominator, has become ruler. Let us rejoice and become ecstatic, and let us give to him the glory; for the marriage of the Lamb has come, and his wife has made herself ready. To her was given [the right] to clothe herself in byssus[-vesture] brilliant and pure; for byssus[-vestures] are the awards to the devotees."

COMMENTARY

Here the main action of the drama is resumed: the chorus, which is the seventh and last, is a pæan of victory following the attainment by the Conqueror of the Spiritual Rebirth. The chorus is chanted by all the powers of the microcosmic universe, the enthroned Logos being the chorus-leader. The word *Hallêlouia,* which is not found elsewhere in the *New Testament,* is here chanted four times.

The marriage (*gamos*) was one of the symbolic rites in the Greek Mysteries; and universally in mysticism spirit is represented as the male, and matter as the female principle. Here the "bride" of the Conqueror is the solar body—the "fire-body" of the Initiate.

Byssus was a fine cloth, naturally of a yellow color, affected by oriental devotees. It represents the auric color of a saintly man.

CH. XIX. 9, 10

And to me [the Divinity] says:

"Write: Immortal are they who are invited to the wedding dinner of the Lamb."

And [again] he says to me:

"These arcane doctrines are the God's."

I fell down before his feet to worship him; but he says to me:

"See to it [that you do] not. I am a fellow-slave with you, and with your brothers who have the evidence of Iêsous. Worship the God."

(For the evidence of Iêsous is the "Breath" of seership.)

COMMENTARY

Absolute certainty of the divine, immortal nature, the conscious spiritual Self, can be had only through the sacred trance, in which all the lower faculties are placed in abeyance, the clamor of the senses, emotions and thoughts completely stilled, so that in the perfect peace and silence of the soul the voice of the inner Self may become audible. This trance-state can be attained only through the action of the *speirêma*, the dynamic working-force of the *paraklêtos*, or "advocate," who pleads with the Father.

CH. XIX. 11–16

I saw the sky opened; and, Behold! a white horse [appeared], and he who was riding him is called Believable and True, and with justice he judges and gives battle. His eyes are like a blaze of fire, and on his head are many diadems; and [on his forehead] he has a name written which no one knows save himself. He is clothed in a garment dyed with blood; and his name is called "The Logos of the God." The armies in the sky were following him, on white horses, wearing byssus[-robes], white and pure. From his mouth keeps flashing forth a keen sword, that with it he might chastise the people. *He* shall rule them with an iron wand. *He* is treading the wine-vat [overflowing with] the wine of the ardor of the passion of the God, the All-Dominator. He has on his garment and on his thigh the name written, "Ruler of rulers and Master of masters."

COMMENTARY

The hero on the white horse is the Second Logos, the incarnating Ego; and he is now the Conqueror, who by indomitable will has completed the telestic work, and is no longer the *inverted* Logos. For here he wears the aspect of Mars, the War-God, who in the older mythology is the God of Generation; he rules with a rod of iron, the metal of Mars; he treads the wine-vat of regenerative force, and he has his title written on his thigh—an euphemism for *phallos,* as in *Old Testament* usage (*Gen.* xxvi. 2, *et passim*). This means that the Conqueror has attained the state of sinless purity, having eradicated from his nature everything that relates to the lower phases of physical existence. He now goes forth to the final battle with the elemental self, the Tartarean ghost of his now defunct psycho-material personality.

CH. XIX. 17, 18

I saw a lone Divinity standing in the sun. He cried out with a great voice, saying to all the birds [of prey] that fly in mid-sky:

"Come! Flock together to the dinner of the great God, so that you may devour the flesh of rulers, the flesh of commanders, the flesh of strong [warriors], the flesh of horses and of their riders, and the flesh of all, free and slave, both small and great."

COMMENTARY

The "lone" Divinities are the Chief-Divinities (*archangeloi*), corresponding to the *Zôa;* here the one standing in the Sun is Mikael, he who drove the Dragon from the sky.

The elemental self is the essence of impurity in the psychic and material elements; and as a sort of by-product, so to say, of the evolutionary æon, it is a concretion of all that was evil in each incarnation during the æonian sojourn of the Ego in the spheres of generation: it is therefore the "flesh," or carnal element, of kings, warriors and all the other personalities assumed by the incarnating Self in the drama being enacted by humanity.

CH. XIX. 19–21

I saw the Beast, and the rulers of the earth and their armies, drawn together to do battle with the Rider on the White Horse and his army. The Beast was captured, and with him the Pseudo-Seer who made the omens in his sight, by which he deluded those who had received the brand of the Beast, and the worshippers of his image. The two [beasts] were cast alive into the lake of fire which flames with sulphur; and the rest were slain by the sword of the Rider on the White Horse, [by the sword] which kept flashing forth from his mouth; and all the birds [of prey] were gorged with their flesh.

COMMENTARY

The battles in the *Apocalypse* are described very briefly, as short and decisive conflicts, and never as protracted struggles. In this one, the instinctual and phrênic principles of the elemental congeries are apprehended and thrown into the astral fire of the phantasmal world, where dissolution is their ultimate fate.

CHAPTER XX. 1–3

I saw a Divinity coming down from the sky, having the key of the abyss and a great chain in his hand. He apprehended the Dragon, the archaic Snake, who is the Accuser and the Adversary, and enchained him for a thousand years, and cast him into the abyss, and locked and sealed [it] atop of him, so that he should not delude the people any more until the thousand years should be finished; and after that he must be turned loose for a short time.

COMMENTARY

Since the hero of the *Apocalypse* is represented as being in the sixth incarnation of the seven making up the cycle of initiation, he has one more earth-life to undergo, and therefore can not yet completely destroy the epithumetic principle; instead, it is placed in durance for a thousand years, after which it must be freed, when the hero reincarnates, whereupon it will be speedily exterminated. This seventh incarnation is the last of the seven rulers who are the seven heads of the Dragon; and of this ruler it is said that "when he does come he must abide a little while." In placing the time between incarnations at a thousand years Iôannês follows Plato, who gives that period, as in *Phaidros*, p. 249, and in the *Republic,* p. 615; in the latter, however, where he is relating the allegory of Er, Plato explains that, owing to the tenfold intensity of sensation in the subjective after-death state, "the thousand years answer to the hundred years which are reckoned as the lifetime of man."

CH. XX. 4–6

I saw thrones and those seated on them; and judgment was passed on them. And [I saw] the souls of those who had been beheaded on account of the evidence of Iêsous and on account of the arcane doctrine of the God; also those who did not worship the Beast or his image, and did not receive his brand on their forehead and on their hand, and they came to life and ruled with the Anointed for a thousand years; [but] the rest of the dead did not come to life again until the thousand years were finished. This is the first resurrection. Immortal and holy is he who has part in the first resurrection; over these the second death does not hold sway, but they shall be sacrificers to the God and his Anointed, and they shall rule with him for the thousand years.

COMMENTARY

When the Beast and the Pseudo-Seer were cast into the astral fire, and the Dragon was incarcerated in the abyss, they made their final exit from the

Apocalyptic stage. The Conqueror has annihilated the bogus Lion and the bogus Lamb; but in his next incarnation he will have to fight and destroy the Dragon, the bogus Archê-Logos. Yet the Apocalyptic drama covers but the one incarnation; and so, rather than leave in uncertainty the issue of the final combat between the Conqueror and the Dragon, Iôannês here introduces a side-scene in which he first explains in a general way what happens to the soul of a man during the periods between incarnations, and then, carrying into the future the story of the Conqueror, describes the final battle in the next incarnation, resulting in the defeat and destruction of the Dragon.

The thrones and those enthroned on them represent a typical individual in a series of incarnations, after each of which, upon the death of the physical body, the enthroned Self passes judgment upon the deeds and misdeeds, on the planes of thought, emotion and action, of the lower self during the preceding earth-life. All the pure and noble thoughts, sentiments, aspirations and memories are retained and remain in the deathless Mind, the Nous, throughout the season of subjective peace and bliss which the soul then experiences; but all the worthless and evil elements are rejected and left to remain dormant in the lower psychic realm, dying the "second death," and coming to life only when the soul again descends into the spheres of generation. Thus the man's own past is his personal "Satan" and "Devil," the ancient serpent trailing through the ages and accusing him day and night before his inner God, who is his righteous Judge.

CH. XX. 7–10

When the thousand years are finished, the Adversary shall be turned loose from his prison and shall come out to delude the people who are in the four corners of the earth (the Gog and Magog), to bring them together for battle, the number of whom is as the sand of the sea. They went up on the width of the earth and surrounded the fortress of the devotees, and the beloved city. And fire came down out of the sky and consumed them. The Accuser, the deluder of them, was thrown into the lake of fire and sulphur, where also are the Beast and the Pseudo-Seer; and they shall be tormented day and night throughout the æons of the æons.

COMMENTARY

Here is foretold the fate of the Dragon, the epithumetic principle, whose host of desires, passions and longings is indeed as the sand of the sea. But they have now no lodging-place in the purified nature of the Conqueror, and exist only as surviving impressions and impulses impressed like phonographic records on the plastic world-soul, and as a malignant composite spectral entity they assail him from without. The purifying fire obliterates these collective phantoms; and their focal centre, the Dragon in his capacity as the "eighth," shares the doom of the bogus Lion and the bogus Lamb. The clause put in parentheses is evidently some scholiast's marginal gloss that has crept into the text, a mere memorandum referring to "Gog" and "Magog," instead of being written out in full as "Gog, king of the land of Magog." It is a true parallel, however, from the Jewish mythology, and indicates that whoever wrote it understood to some extent the esoteric meaning of the *Apocalypse* and also the inner sense of the *Old Testament* myths. In fact, no real esotericist could possibly fail to perceive the general meaning of the Apocalyptic allegory; and the solution of its peculiar puzzles calls only for the exercise of ingenuity on the part of any one "who has the Nous." But through the ages the esotericists have merely smiled and remained silent while the exoteric "Fathers of the Church" and their worthy successors have tortured this magnificent epic into a theological nightmare; for if the "orthodox" had discovered its real nature, the *Apocalypse* would unquestionably have shared the fate of the learned Porphyry's treatise on Christianity, which was burned by decree of the Roman Emperor.

CH. XX. 11–15

I saw a great white throne and [the God] seated on it, from whose face fled the earth and the sky—and a place was not found for them. I saw the dead, the great and the small, standing before the throne; and [their] scrolls were unrolled. Another scroll was unrolled, which is [the Lamb's scroll] of life. The dead were judged from the [records] written in [their] scrolls, according to their works. The sea gave up the dead which were in it, and Death and the Unseen gave the dead which were in them; and they were judged every one according to their works. Death and the Unseen were thrown into the lake of fire. This is the second death—the lake of fire. If any one was not found registered in the [Lamb's] scroll of life, he was thrown into the lake of fire.

COMMENTARY

Here the action of the drama is again resumed. The initiate has severed himself from the lower life, and by thus renouncing everything pertaining to the generated form of existence he is morally and dynamically in the same condition as is the disincarnated man, so that his past must be adjudicated in the same way. But, whereas the after-death judgment of the uninitiated soul involves only its last preceding earth-life, the Conqueror must render an account of all his past incarnations: the records in their scrolls are reviewed, and then all are summed up in the Lamb's great scroll of life—the comprehensive record of the incarnating Self. All his deeds in the great sea of sensuous life, all the things that he ever did in the physical and psychic worlds, spring to life in the Eternal Memory, and all are passed upon by the inexorable Judge, and whatever element in the æon-evolved character of the man that is found unworthy of life eternal is hurled into the consuming fire of the chaos, there to disintegrate in the second death. In this there is no shadow of that exoteric and profane notion, the "vicarious atonement." According to the philosophy of Iôannês, Seer and Initiate, the great Teacher of the Christian cycle, rigid justice rules all worlds.

CHAPTER XXI. 1–5

I saw a new sky and a new earth—for the first sky and the first earth have passed away, and the sea *is* not any more. I saw the holy city, New Hierousalêm, coming down out of the sky—from the God—made ready as a bride bedecked for her husband. I heard a great voice from the throne, saying:

"Behold! the tent of the God is with men, and he shall pitch tent with them. *They* shall be his people and the God himself shall be with them—*their* God! He shall wipe away every tear from their eyes; and there shall not be death any more, nor shall there be mourning, lamentation or pain any more. For the material elements have passed away."

Said the [Master] seated on the throne:

"Behold! I am making a new universe."

And to me he says:

"Write: These arcane doctrines are believable and true."

COMMENTARY

In the prelude to the first act of the drama (iv. 11) the Powers chant a pæan to the God who brought into existence the universe; but now that microcosmic "universe," the lower self which had been evolved during the generative æons, has fulfilled its purpose, and is superceded by a new Universe, a new cycle of spiritual evolution transcendent in glory.

CH. XXI. 6–8

And [again] he said to me:

"He has been *born,* [but] *I* am the Alpha and the Ô, the Origin and the Perfection. To him who thirsts *I* shall give of the spring of the water of life as a free gift. THE CONQUEROR shall obtain the universe, and I will be a God to him, and he shall be a son to me. But, for the cowardly, the unbelieving, the malodorous, murderers, fornicators, sorcerers, worshippers of phantoms, and all liars, their part [shall be] in the lake which flames with fire and sulphur—which is the second death."

COMMENTARY

The First Logos, the enthroned God, who is the source of life and its ultimate goal, is never incarnated; the Second Logos is the incarnating Self; and the man as he is on earth is the Third Logos, who, if he conquers and achieves the second birth, becomes the son of the God. Yet the three are in reality one, the Divine Man manifested on three planes of life. Nevertheless, if the carnal man becomes irredeemably wicked, his fate is the second death, the reverse of the second birth: his psychic self decomposes in the fiery subtile elements, even as the physical body is resolved into its original elements when abandoned by the animating principle. The second death means the obliteration of the personal consciousness; the second birth leads to the attuning of the individual consciousness with that which is universal and divine.

A variant reading in the text has "I have been born," but the *gegone* of the received text is preferable. The revisers have adopted the extraordinary reading *gegonan*, from which they extract the almost meaningless statement, "They are come to pass."

CH. XXI. 9–14

Came one of the seven Divinities who had the seven libation-saucers, who were charged with the seven last scourges, and he talked with me, saying:

"Hither! I shall show you the bride—the Lamb's wife."

He carried me away in the Breath[-trance] to a mountain great and high, and showed me the holy city Hierousalêm, coming down out of the sky from the God, having the God's glory—[and this], her luminary, was like a very precious stone, like an opal crystal-glittering—having a wall great and high; having twelve gateways, and at the gateways twelve Divinities, and [on the gateways] names inscribed, which are [the names] of the twelve tribes of the children of Israel: on the east were three gateways, on the north three gateways, on the south three gateways, and on the west three gateways. The wall of the city had twelve foundations, and on them [were inscribed] the twelve names of the twelve apostles of the Lamb.

COMMENTARY

The mountains of the *Apocalypse* are the *chakras* and the states of consciousness to which they correspond; the symbolism is almost universal, and many were the ancient cities having their seven sacred mountains, or hills. The *Book of Enoch* describes seven mountains each of which was composed of one of the seven metals ascribed to the planets. These are: Saturn, lead; Jupiter, tin; Mars, iron; Sun, gold; Venus, copper; Mercury, quicksilver; and Moon, silver.

The *iaspis* is thought by some authorities to have been the diamond or the opal, and the latter supposition is doubtless correct, as the self-luminous aura, the glory, basically white, but coruscating with all the seven colors, resembles a brilliant opal. The aura (the wall of the city) has twelve force-centres, where the twelve cosmic forces (the apostles of the Lamb, or Sun) are focussed upon the microcosm, and these focal centres are dynamically related to the twelve orifices of the body—the twelve gateways of the city, corresponding to the twelve tribes. Thus, quite literally, even on the plane of forces, the Conqueror obtains the Universe.

CH. XXI. 15–21

The [Divinity] who was talking with me had for a measure a golden reed, to measure the city, its gateways and its wall. The city lies foursquare, and its length is as great as its width. He measured the city with the reed, by *stadia,* twelve thousand; its length, width and height are equal. And he measured its wall, one hundred and forty-four cubits, [including] the measure of a man, that is, of a Divinity. The building-material of its wall was opal, and the city was pure gold, like clear glass. The foundations of the wall of the city were ornamented with every precious stone: the first foundation was opal; the second, sapphire; the third, chalcedony; the fourth, aqua-marine; the fifth, sardonyx; the sixth, carnelian; the seventh, chrysolite; the eighth, beryl; the ninth, topaz; the tenth, chrysoprase; the eleventh, jacinth; and the twelfth, amethyst. The twelve gateways were twelve pearls: each one of the twelve gateways was [carved] from a single pearl.

COMMENTARY

As already explained, the cubical city, when unfolded, becomes a cross, symbolizing the human form. It is the solar body, *to sôma hêliakon,* the numerical value of the words being 1,600, the number of Jewish miles in 12,000 *stadia.* The Roman mile of about eight *stadia,* it should be noted, was never used by the Jews, who counted seven and a half *stadia* to the mile. The aura, *hê doxa,* gives the number 143, to which is added an *alpha,* 1, that being the vowel and number of the primeval man, or Divinity.

The aura is a brilliant opalescence, self-luminous, and the solar body has the appearance of transparent gold.

The twelve precious stones are not all identified with certainty, as some of the Greek names are dubious; but, given in the modern terms generally applied to them, they are probably as follows: 1, opal; 2, lapis-lazuli; 3, chalcedony; 4, aqua-marine; 5, sardonyx; 6, carnelian; 7, topaz; 8, beryl; 9, chrysolith; 10, chrysoprase; 11, hyacinth; and 12, amethyst. Placed in a circle, as if incorporated in the aura, these colored stones form approximately the prismatic scale, and are thus identical with the rainbow (iv. 3) which encircles the throne of the God.

CH. XXI. 21–27

The main-street of the city was pure gold, transparent as glass. No adytum did I see in it; for the Master-God, the All-Dominator, and the Lamb are its adytum. The city has no need of the sun, nor of the moon, to shine in it; for the God's glory lights it up; and its lamp is the Lamb, and the people [who are of the delivered] shall walk in its light; and the rulers of the earth keep bringing their glory into it. Its gateways shall not at all be closed by day—for there shall be no night there. They shall bring the glory and the honor of the people into it; and there shall not at all enter into it anything profane, or he who creates a stench and [acts] a lie, but only those who are registered in the Lamb's scroll of life.

COMMENTARY

The broad street, or highway, of the solar forces, "the rulers from the Sun's place of birth," corresponds to the spinal cord of the physical body. But the complex structure of the gross form, with the numerous organs and functions made necessary by material conditions, is not duplicated in the spiritual body, which is formed of etheric fire, and is in direct relation with, and is sustained by, the cosmic and divine forces.

CHAPTER XXII. 1–5

He showed me a pure river of the water of life, clear as crystal, flowing out of the throne of the God and of the Lamb, in the middle of its main-street; and on one side of the river and on the other was the tree of life, producing twelve fruits according to the months, each one yielding its fruit; and the leaves of the tree were for the healing of the people—and the accursed [function] shall not exist any more. The throne of the God and of the Lamb shall be in it, and his slaves will serve him;

they will see his face, and his name [will be] on their foreheads. There will be no night there; and they will have no need of lamp or light of the sun: for the Master-God will give them light, and they will rule throughout the æons of the æons.

COMMENTARY

The river of life and the two trees of life correspond to the three *nâdîs;* but, whereas in the physical body the triple current ascends to the brain from below, from the generative centres, in the solar body the "accursed" function, sex, does not exist, and the forces come from above, from the brain-region. In the inverted Logos, the "son of man," the creative centres are the lowest; in the Conqueror, who has become the "Son of the God," they are the highest. The Archê-Logos is the "Witness" and has his "two witnesses," the three constituting the creative triad; therefore he has his name written on his thigh. This is the secret meaning of the Kabalistic maxim, *Demon est Deus inversus.* The generative function is strictly nothing but an animal one, and can never be anything else. True spirituality demands its utter extirpation; and while its proper exercise for the continuation of the human race, in the semi-animal stage of its evolution, may not be considered sinful, its misuse, in any way, is fraught with the most terrible consequences physically, psychically and spiritually; and the forces connected with it are used for abnormal purposes only in the foulest practices of sorcery, the inevitable result of which is moral death—the annihilation of the individuality. The only true creative function is that of the Nous, the Godlike faculty of formative Thought.

CH. XXII. 6–9

He said to me:

"These arcane doctrines are believable and true. The Master-God of the 'Breaths' of the seers sent his Divinity to make known to his slaves the [perfections] which must be attained speedily. Behold! I am coming speedily. Immortal is he who observes the arcane doctrines of the teaching of this scroll."

I, Iôannês, am he who was seeing and hearing these [mysteries]; and when I heard and saw, I fell down to worship before the feet of the Divinity who was making known these [mysteries] to me. And he says to me:

"See to it [that you do] not. I am a *fellow-slave* with you and with your brothers, the seers, and those who observe the arcane doctrines of the teachings of this scroll. Worship the God!"

COMMENTARY

The Breaths (*pneumata*) of the seers are the differentiated forces of the Pneuma, or Great Breath of Life, used by the seers in the telestic work, and are not the "spirits" of ancient worthies. The Arch-Divinity of these creative forces is the Nous.

Nothing should be worshipped that has form or is individuated. The universal Divine Life is alone to be worshipped. There is no colorless pantheism in this concept; for the God of each man is one with the universal God: the Conqueror obtains the Universe, not by being absorbed and obliterated by it, but by transcending the limitations of his individual consciousness and partaking of the universal Divine Consciousness. As an individual he loses nothing but his imperfections, but he gains the All, the "Origin and the Perfection." And this is *Seership,* which is not "prophecy," "second sight," or sense-perception on any plane of consciousness, but is Direct Cognition of Reality.

CH. XXII. 10–16

And [again] he says to me:

"Do not seal up the arcane doctrines of the teachings of this scroll; for the season is near. The unjust, let him do injustice yet more; the sordid, let him be made yet more sordid; the just, let him do justice yet more; and the devotee, let him be made yet more devoted. Behold! I am coming speedily, and my wages are with me, to pay off each [laborer] as his work is. *I* am the Alpha and the Ô, the First [Adam] and the Last [Adam], the Origin and the Perfection. Immortal are those who are washing their robes so that they may have authority over the tree of life and may enter by the gateways into the city. Outside are the dogs, the sorcerers, the fornicators, the murderers, the phantom-servers, and every one who keeps sanctioning and acting a lie. *I*, Iêsous, have sent my Divinity to give evidence to you of these [works depending] upon the Societies. *I* am the Root and the Offspring of David, his bright and Morning Star."

COMMENTARY

The injunction not to seal up the teachings has been followed by the Apocalyptist; for although his scroll is written in veiled language it is not "sealed" as in the case of a strictly occult book, which is written either in cipher or secret language, and can not be read without a key. Mystical works intended for general circulation are usually worded obscurely, being designed to elicit and cultivate the intuitive faculty of the reader; and they are, almost without exception, disconnected, fragmentary, and often interspersed with irrelevant passages. But the *Apocalypse* contains its own key, and is complete in itself, coherent, and scrupulously accurate in every detail. The puzzles it contains are not intended to mislead or confuse; on the contrary, they serve to verify the correct interpretation of the allegory. The book is not sealed to any one who has the developed intuitive faculty, and for whom, therefore, the season, the springtime of noetic unfoldment, is near.

Though the growth of the inner nature is a slow process during many incarnations, the recognition of the actuality of the soul, of the immanent higher mind, comes upon the man suddenly; as Iôannês reiterates, the Logos comes speedily, unexpectedly, as a thief in the night; and when it does come there is a balancing of merits and demerits. If his nature is sufficiently purified, the mystic tree of life (the *speirêma*) is his, and by means of it he enters the holy city; otherwise he remains with "those without," the exotericists, until he shall have "washed his robes" and thereby gained the right to employ the "Breaths of the seers."

The Divinity speaking to Iôannês is one of the septenary group who poured out the libations in the final ordeals; he forbids the seer to worship him, declaring himself to be but a fellow-servitor; then he announces himself as both the First and the Second Logos; and lastly he calls himself Iêsous, the incarnating Self of David. The Initiate has thus "gathered himself together," unifying his whole nature, and correlating his consciousness in the four worlds.

CH. XXII. 17–21

Both the Breath and the Bride are saying, "Come!" Let him who hears say, "Come!" Let him who is athirst come; and let him who is willing receive the water of life as a free gift.

I give corroborative evidence to every one who hears the arcane doctrines of the teaching of this scroll, [and I give warning] that if any one shall add [forgeries] to them, the God will add to him the scourges which are written in this scroll;

and if any one shall erase [any portion] from the arcane doctrines of the scroll of this teaching, the God will erase his portion from the scroll of life and from the holy city, [even from] the [initiations] which are described in this scroll.

He who gives evidence of these [arcane doctrines] says:

"Verily, I am coming speedily."

AMÊN. Come, Master Iêsous!

The Grace of the Master Iêsous be with the devotees. AMÊN.

COMMENTARY

In the days when books could be published only in the form of manuscripts it was comparatively easy for unscrupulous persons to alter them to suit their own views by expunging words and passages and by interpolating forgeries. Religious sectarians were particularly addicted to this form of literary vandalism, as is clearly evident from the mutilated text of portions of the *New Testament,* especially the letters of Paulos. The statement that terrible consequences would result to any one tampering with the text of this scroll of Iôannês has doubtless stayed the hand of many a superstitious bigot, and has operated to preserve it intact; but the warning is more than a mere idle threat, for the man who would maliciously mutilate this manual written for the spiritual guidance of the "little children" of the Logos would find a grave indictment charged against him when he came to be "judged according to his works." That the text has been preserved with remarkable purity is shown by the fact that the puzzles it contains have not been touched, though even slight changes by a meddlesome "redactor" might have ruined them.

Even as the Light of the Logos keeps saying to mankind, "Come," so the learner, he who hears that summons, should repeat the call, tendering as a free gift the water of life to all who thirst for it and are willing to receive it. But woe to those who by attempting to trade in the things of the spirit have lost the key of the Gnôsis, leaving themselves locked out and hindering those who were ready to enter!

Now, the Master Iêsous is the Spiritual Mind of man, which alone can give absolute proof of the truth of the Life Eternal; and he indeed comes swiftly to those who make themselves pure and become worthy to utter the word of power—the AMÊN.

Printed in the USA
CPSIA information can be obtained
at www.ICGtesting.com
LVHW021300120823
755037LV00011B/1226